HIGHER
History

grade **booster**

✕ John A Kerr ✕

Text © John Kerr
Design and layout © 2010 Leckie & Leckie
Cover image © Burçin Yildirim

03/111012

All rights reserved. No part of this publication may be reproduced, stored in a
retrieval system, or transmitted in any form or by any means, electronic, mechanical,
photocopying, recording or otherwise, without prior permission in writing from Leckie
& Leckie Ltd. Legal action will be taken by Leckie & Leckie Ltd against any infringement
of our copyright.

The right of John Kerr to be identified as author of this Work has been asserted by him
in accordance with sections 77 and 78 of the Copyright, Designs and Patents Act 1988.

ISBN 978-1-84372-729-3

Published by
Leckie & Leckie Ltd
An imprint of HarperCollinsPublishers
Westerhill Road, Bishopbriggs, Glasgow, G64 2QT
T: 0844 576 8126   F: 0844 576 8131
leckieandleckie@harpercollins.co.uk   www.leckieandleckie.co.uk

Special thanks to
documen (design and page makeup),
Jennifer Richards (proofreading)
Jill Laidlaw (Copy-editing)

A CIP Catalogue record for this book is available from the British Library.

Leckie & Leckie makes every effort to ensure that all paper used in its books is made
from wood pulp obtained from well-managed forests, controlled sources and recycled
wood or fibre.

Acknowledgements
We would like to thank the following for permission to reproduce their material:
Birlinn Ltd for an extract from People and Society in Scotland Vol II, 1830-1914 by
W. Hamish Fraser and R. J. Morris reproduced by kind permission of Birlinn Ltd
www.birlinn.co.uk (p.59).
Scran Limited for poster on p.79 © Dumfries and Galloway Council.
Licensor www.scran.ac.uk

Every effort has been made to trace the copyright holders and to obtain their
permission for the use of copyright material. Leckie & Leckie will gladly receive
information enabling them to rectify any error or omission in subsequent editions.

MIX
Paper from
responsible sources
FSC™ C007454

FSC™ is a non-profit international organisation established to promote
the responsible management of the world's forests. Products carrying the
FSC label are independently certified to assure consumers that they come
from forests that are managed to meet the social, economic and
ecological needs of present and future generations,
and other controlled sources.

Find out more about HarperCollins and the environment at
www.harpercollins.co.uk/green

CONTENTS

Introduction

What's in this book?

What will this book help me to do?

How should I use this book?

Must I try all the examples of questions?

Will this book tell me all the facts I need for the exam?

WHAT'S IN THIS BOOK?

Chapter 1 focuses on the Extended Essay. You will write an Extended Essay a few weeks before the main exam so this chapter will give you the best possible start towards gaining a very good grade at Higher History.

Chapter 2 focuses on Higher Paper 1 in which you will be asked to write two essays. The chapter is divided into sections on writing introductions, developing your essay and reaching – and writing – conclusions. There is also advice about how your essays will be marked.

Chapter 3 explains how to develop the different skills you need to deal with the four different types of questions you will be asked in Higher Paper 2.

WHAT WILL THIS BOOK HELP ME TO DO?

You will learn how to achieve the best possible grades at Higher level. You will learn how to answer the different types of question you will be asked. You will find lots of advice and examples of answers – both good and bad – so that you can improve your skills.

HOW SHOULD I USE THIS BOOK?

The short answer is when you need it! This book is not meant to be read all at once. In fact, you may find some parts of the book scary if they deal with sections of the course you have not yet started. But when you are working on the Extended Essay or checking how to write essays or how to prepare Paper 2 answers, turn to the relevant section and use it to help you get the best possible results.

MUST I TRY ALL THE EXAMPLES OF QUESTIONS?

No. This book contains examples from the most popular topics but no student studies all the topics. Find the ones that apply to you.

WILL THIS BOOK TELL ME ALL THE FACTS I NEED FOR THE EXAM?

This book will NOT tell you all the information you need for your Higher History course. All that can be found in two other books from Leckie & Leckie called *Higher History Course Notes*, Books 1 and 2.

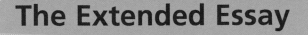

1 | The Extended Essay

Introduction

Choosing my essay title

Planning my essay

Writing my essay

Exam example

Marking

INTRODUCTION

At some point in your higher course you will be asked to write an Extended Essay. It usually takes place in the spring, about two or three months before the final exam.

What is the Extended Essay?

Your teachers and the SQA know that you are unlikely to show your best possible work in an exam that only allows you 40 minutes to write an essay. That is why the Extended Essay was introduced. By choosing your own title, having time to research and prepare and then having 2 hours to write up your essay you have a chance to create an essay that shows your best work. In the words of the SQA, the Extended Essay is a *'top of the range version of what a candidate is capable of given research and writing time'*.

Why is the Extended Essay important to me?

It is really important to do as well as you can in the Extended Essay because the mark you get forms part of your final Higher exam award total. In fact, the Extended Essay counts for 30 marks out of a total of 100 so doing well in the

Extended Essay can provide you with a very useful launch pad for future success. The average mark for Extended Essays is just over 18 out of 30 – that's a B! You can achieve more than that.

How long does my essay have to be?

The answer is simple – what you can write in 2 hours! There are NO word limits in the Extended Essay. Most people can write one page of A4 in 10 minutes. Since there are 12 x 10 minutes in 2 hours it is possible to write a twelve page essay and some students write more. The usual length of an essay is about seven or eight pages. Very short essays start alarm bells ringing in the heads of markers given that students have had time to prepare and practice, but each essay is read and marked on its merits.

CHOOSING MY ESSAY TITLE

Should I try to choose a title that is fresh and new and different?

No, it's not necessary and choosing an essay title that is deliberately different from any other could cause you problems. Some candidates disadvantage themselves by selecting inappropriate titles for their essays. Ask your teacher or tutor if you are unsure.

Are there rules about the title that I can choose?

Yes, there are two main rules.

 Your essay topic must be part of the syllabus you are studying. So an essay about the military campaigns of World War Two would risk gaining 0 marks since it is not within the Higher syllabus. Your essay title MUST be part of the Higher History syllabus. Check this at: http://www.sqa.org.uk/sqa/files_ccc/History_Higher_2010.pdf

 Your essay title must be issue-based and not simply descriptive. In other words, there must be an issue or question within your title such as ' "Appeasement was the only possible policy for Britain to follow when dealing with Nazi Germany."

How valid is that opinion?' or 'How successful was the Labour Government of 1945–51 in dealing with the social problems facing Britain after World War Two?' or 'To what extent was German unification inevitable with or without Bismarck?'

A good way to check if your essay is issue-based is to look for the question mark at the end of the title. If your essay has no question mark at the end – such as 'Appeasement' or 'The Crusades Fail' or 'The Tsar, 1917' or 'Bismarck and the Unification of Germany' then you are likely to get less than half marks. That's because the marker has no way of knowing what you are trying to do apart from simply writing a description of the subject in the title. However, if your title is a definite question then your essay should be OK, as it will hopefully answer this question!

Are there types of questions to avoid?

Yes! Weaknesses are most often displayed in particular types of questions.

Double issues

Avoid asking two questions for the price of one. Why give yourself extra work? Bad questions could be:

- 'Why were fascist foreign policies so aggressive and was Munich more a success for Hitler or for Chamberlain?'

OR

- 'Why did the Liberal Reforms happen and how successful were they?'

As a rough guide, avoid the word 'AND' in your title.

Questions that are phrased in such a way that makes their meanings unclear or lack focus

Sometimes a title can make it hard for the marker to know what the student is trying to argue, such as:

- 'Was Rowntree the nagging conscience of the Liberals?' (The candidate really wanted to answer a question about the causes of the Liberal Reforms.)

OR

- 'Was Lenin the cork bobbing on the tide of revolution or was he the driving force behind the wave?' (In other words 'How important was Lenin to the Russian Revolution of Nov 1917?')

What types of questions are good styles to choose?

Please notice that this title contains the word STYLES. The following are examples of questions that you could adapt to fit in with your preference for a topic. Look at past papers, either in shops or on the SQA website. There is no reason why you can't choose a past paper question. That way you know the question is acceptable to the SQA!

Here are some examples of suitable styles of questions.

From Church, State and Feudal Society

'The lives of peasants in the Middle Ages were dominated by fear, ignorance and superstition.' How accurate is that view?

From The Century of Revolutions 1603–1702

'Charles I's attempt to impose his authority in Scotland was a failure.' How valid is that view?

From Britain 1851–1951

How important was the example of municipal socialism in persuading the Liberal Government to introduce social reforms between 1906 and 1914?

From Germany 1815–1939

How important were cultural factors in the growth of national feeling in Germany between 1815 and 1850?

From USA 1918–1968

How successful was the New Deal in solving the social and economic problems of the USA in the 1930s?

From Appeasement and the Road to War, to 1939

How far did appeasement achieve its aims up to March 1938?

Can I write an essay based on my Paper 2 Special Topic?

Yes, you can. There are advantages and disadvantages. You will not have any past essay titles to give you ideas to choose from. Since there is no essay question in Paper 2 you will not have the chance of being lucky and seeing your Extended Essay title cropping up in the final exam. However, both the 'How fully' and the 'How far' questions are just mini essays demanding quite a bit of recall. Also, you must have covered and revised ALL main and sub-issues in your Paper 2 topic because all the issues will be examined in some way. You know that recall is important in your Paper 2 answers, so an extended essay would certainly make sure you had covered at least one of the issues thoroughly.

What if my Extended Essay title appears in the final exam?

You just got lucky! If you choose your Extended Essay from mainstream titles it is quite possible that your topic, and perhaps even a title similar to your Extended Essay, will appear in the final exam. There are NO restrictions on answering that question based on the knowledge you gained or indeed your memory of the structure you used and the analysis points you made in your Extended Essay. But be careful to adapt your information to fit the exact question asked in the exam.

Can I do the same title as my friend?

Yes you can but, before you do, think carefully. Is your whole class doing the same title? That might not be a good idea. The SQA is concerned about lots of essays coming from the same centres with the same titles. Such patterns can result from students choosing a title that has been the subject of a class lesson on planning an essay. That approach can help weaker candidates gain confidence by providing a structure to their essay but if you have ambitions to do well then it is always best to do your own work, based of course on advice from your teachers and your experience from earlier essays.

PLANNING MY ESSAY

What is the Extended Essay plan?

Your plan provides a framework for your essay. You are allowed up to 200 words in your plan. The plan shows markers that you have researched, selected and organised information. It also gives you a chance to lay out your essay in a rough format that outlines the main stages in

your essay and include important factual information and ideas. Your Extended Essay plan MUST be sent to the SQA with your finished essay, preferably on the official form downloadable from the SQA website at www.sqa.org.uk. Remember to include a word count in the box provided. However, your plan can be spread over as many pages as you like if it helps you. Just attach it to the official form.

Is the plan really a plan?

This depends on you. Your 'plan' is really more of a summary of your essay which will help to remind you of its flow when you finally write it under exam conditions. The most important thing about your plan is that it should help you to write the best possible essay you can.

Most candidates alter their plan several times before the final write-up. Once you have a plan, it is always a good idea to find time to practice writing your essay with only the plan to help you. That way, if you miss anything out, you can fix the plan to remind you of the forgotten material you want to include in your essay. You might also be able to show your plan to your teachers and tutors for them to offer advice, although they are not obliged to do so.

Will my plan be marked?

The plan is NOT marked but it is a vital part of your essay both for your use and for markers to see that you have completed the required planning stage. Nor is there any time limit to writing your plan. The plan is YOURS. You can change it, colour it or print it out. You can write it anywhere, anytime before you write your Extended Essay under exam conditions. However if you want your teacher to look over your plan then it would be wise to negotiate with him or her when your plan should be ready to look at.

Are there any rules about the plan?

Yes, there is one absolute rule. The SQA reported, *'Centres should remind candidates of the 200 word limit for the Extended Essay.'* So your plan must NOT be longer than 200 words. You WILL have marks deducted from your final essay mark if you go over that limit. Don't take the chance.

Are diagrams and pictures allowed in the plan?

No. The SQA are aware of some people trying to get round the rules by using code words or pictograms. The SQA's position on this is clear. *'Pictograms, maps, codes and text language will be penalised.'* If it is felt that candidates are trying to get round the rules of the Extended Essay they will lose marks. However, diagrams such as mind maps are acceptable. The SQA guidance states, *'mind maps and colour to enhance the organisation of the plan are permissible'*. After all, mind maps are just words organised with boxes and lines and colour around them. However, ways of increasing the number of words, such as using small drawings or cartoons in the plan, are dealt with seriously – and watch out for the words you write on your mind map. They are also counted as part of your 200 words.

Can I use abbreviations?

Yes, but what's the point? Each abbreviation will still be counted as a word so abbreviations will not reduce the total number of words. However common abbreviations such as KKK, TVA and NHS are counted as one word, not three.

How should I write and use my plan?

Your plan should be exactly that – a plan of the essay you will write. Your plan should NOT be just a collection of facts, figures and quotes. It is NOT a random selection of research notes. It is a PLAN!

Even without the actual essay in front of him or her, a marker should be able to see what your essay structure would be, what main ideas you would include and the sequence they would follow, just by looking at your plan. After all, your plan is meant to help you by reminding you what should be in your essay.

A few people write their essay 'fresh' in the exam room, using their plan as help. That means they have not written the essay before. This is not recommended.

Most people will have written their Extended Essay several times before they write the real Extended Essay in exam conditions. By doing this, you have several advantages. First of all you allow yourself a chance to rethink and edit your work. You can choose to word process or hand-write at this stage. Word processed work is easier to change by cutting and pasting, spell checking and so on, but handwriting is good practice for the time you will have in the exam and also, by writing it over again, you will establish the essay in your memory.

Secondly, once your draft has been written you may be able to get a teacher or tutor to read over your essay and make suggestions.

Finally, when you have written the essay two or three times you will have a fairly clear idea of what you will write and how long it will take you. Now you must condense the essentials of your essay into a 200 word plan.

How should I organise my plan?

Since your **introduction** is vital, you could have it written out in condensed form but as close to the real thing as possible. You could use about sixty or seventy words for this. Your outline introduction could also include the main ideas and themes that you will develop later. The SQA recommends an approach like this when it states, '*Many candidates merely produce a "story" in the Extended Essay. An analytical approach assisted by the use of a clear plan to provide a clear structure to the essay would have assisted such "average" candidates.*'

Moving on to the main body of your essay, you could aim to write a series of key sentences that would start off each paragraph – although a well-written introduction should outline what each paragraph will be about.

If you are intending to write about eight paragraphs, each one in your plan should be allocated ten words. That means you will use about eighty words.

Remember that you should use supporting evidence throughout your essay. History skills should run throughout the essay. That means you must not only use factual detail but also be prepared to use quotes and make reference, if you can, to the reliability and accuracy of the information used. If you are using quotes, do not waste words copying them out fully in your plan. Each quote should be boiled down to essential words to prompt you.

It is also helpful to remind yourself to include mini conclusions linking each paragraph back to the main title so you keep your arguments going and don't fall back into storytelling with little connection to the main question.

Finally you must have a strong **conclusion**. It is really important to summarise your main ideas and prioritise your information to arrive at a direct, balanced answer to the main question. You might want to write out the skeleton of your conclusion and if you have followed the word allocation so far you will have at least fifty words for this. That's about six lines of normal writing! So you could really work on your conclusion and have most of it in your plan. And remember – try to ensure your conclusion ends on a high note, perhaps with an appropriate quote that provides an overall answer to the question or which supports your main argument.

Is there anything else I can do to prepare effectively?

The layout of your plan can be made to work for you. Lay out the plan clearly for you to see what is going where and in what order.

What does a weak essay plan and a better essay plan look like?

The first plan is based around the title:

> Why did Robert the Bruce succeed in gaining Scottish independence while others had failed?

PLAN (If your plan exceeds 200 words in length you may lose up to 10 marks)

<u>Wallace</u>

Stirling bridge

Guardianship not noble – no support

Falkirk escaped abroad

Guerilla warfare

Diplomacy

<u>English weakness</u>

Wars on three fronts:Scotland, France + Wales

<u>Church/diplomacy</u>

Declaration of the clergy 1309 – acknowledgement of Bruce, denounced Balliol

Declaration of Arbroath 1320 letter to Pope

Supported Wallace + Bruce

<u>Unconquerable scotland</u>

Geographically uncontrollable due to mountains, hills, etc

Small communities

<u>Robert Bruce</u>

Bannockburn

Raids to Northern England

Roxburgh

Scottish Independence/Treaty of Northampton 1328

St Andrews

<u>Conclusion</u>

Round up all sections evenly + come to balanced conclusion

Why is this a weak plan?

The plan is too short. You are allowed 200 words so why not use them all to your advantage? This plan is only about ninety words.

There are at least some headings but the plan is mainly a list of facts, names and events. There is no reminder about ideas or the argument that is implicit in the title.

Remember your essay is about an issue that should be debated. That means different points of view should be included and there should be a theme or argument running through your essay supporting your ideas. In this case, what were the reasons for Bruce succeeding where others had failed? There are no suggestions of reasons in this plan.

The real indication of just how weak this essay plan is lies in the conclusion: you know already that introductions and conclusions are vital to an essay. This plan has neither. It goes straight into a list of facts suggesting this candidate has just not thought through what should be in the essay. Essentially, the plan for the conclusion translates as 'write a conclusion' – not a very helpful comment!

The next plan is better. It is based around the following title:

To what extent was Bismarck responsible for the unification of Germany?

PLAN (If your plan exceeds 200 words in length you may lose up to 10 marks)

Intro	– Bismarck
	– Minister President
	– 'Blood and Iron'
	– 'Played cards well, but did not deal them'
	– Diplomacy
	– 3 Wars
	– 1871
Other factors	– Cultural
	– Economic
	– Political

Development	– Pre Bismarck
	– Political
	– French Revolution, Napoleon, 400 - 39 Confederation Rhine
	– Liberalism and Nationalism ideas spreading
	– 1815 – Reaction, Metternich, Carlsbad Decrees – German Confederation not move to unity
	– 1848 – Frankfurt Parliament – hopes failures
	– 1850 Olmutz
Cultural	– Fichte – Nationalist unity against common enemy
	– Student Societies
	– Wartburg Festival
	– Beethoven, Grimm Bros
	– Watch on Rhine 1830s
Economic	– 'Mighty Lever German unification' – Zollverein – prototype Kleindeutsch
	– Railway network – Prussian centred
	– No unity by 1860s
	– Bismarck
	– Achieves political stability and authority in Prussia – Landtag issue
	– War 1 Denmark – Schleswig Holstein – Austria – Gastein. Benefit Prussia
	– War 2 – Austria – diplomatic preparation – isolation Austria – Russia, Italy, France – Sadowa Prague
	– North German Confederation
	– War 3 – France – Ems Telegram – Sedan – Versailles – Unification or Prussianisation?
Conclusion	– "Not by majority verdicts but blood and iron. Used tools already in place – Prussian army reformed, rail network, industrial muscle. Coincidences – Hohenzollern candidate, Italian nationalist struggle, Crimean war and relationship with Russia.
	– Unlikely German unification happened if B had not existed.

Why is this a better plan?

The answer should already be clear to you. It uses all of the allocation. There is a structure with a clear introduction, development and conclusion. There are facts but also ideas which will help with analysis. There is a conclusion which sums up the main argument outlined in the introduction.

However, be aware that although this is an acceptable plan it's not perfect. There are few reminders of the different views of historians (called historiography). The introduction is still weak, however there is enough here to remind the writer of the main points, and if the points are developed well, the candidate should get into the B range of marks.

Finally, a word about language and style. The SQA gives explicit advice. *'Candidates should not use informal casual style such as "In this essay I hope to..." or "In my conclusion I have shown that ...". At Higher level a more formal and mature style of writing is expected.'* In other words DO NOT USE these phrases or phrases like them. Try to write in a clear adult style avoiding slang terms, vague generalisations and text language.

WRITING MY ESSAY

Must I include lots of quotes from historians?

The SQA recently reported, 'Many candidates showed good knowledge and understanding of historical content and in some cases there was also evidence of awareness of historical debate and the use of historiography.' It continued, *'There are signs of some candidates developing a number of skills including research into a variety of sources, awareness of historical debate and historiography, selective and constructive use of quotations from historical sources. All of these contributed to well structured essays.'*

Do I need to know what historiography is?

Yes. History is about researching and explaining the past and that is what historians do. Historiography is the study of historians and their views. Often, historians have different opinions, so by using your knowledge of these differing points of view, you will be able to give a more effective, debate-type answer.

Including quotes to support your ideas can also help to improve your answer but remember to credit those quotes with the author's name.

But beware! Avoid using trivial 'quotes' to create a bogus impression of real research. For example, one candidate wrote, 'World War broke out in 1914 (A.J.P.Taylor)'. Any quotes you use should express the point of view of the author and if possible be contrasted with a differing point from another source. One word of warning – 'invented' or 'made up' quotes usually stick out like sore thumbs. They are easily spotted and punished!

So to summarise, if your essay takes an issue and looks at different viewpoints and differing interpretations of what happened and why it happened then you are likely to do well.

Must I include quotes to get an A award?

It is NOT TRUE to think an A grade award is impossible without quotes from named historians. Every year many candidates get A awards because they use information accurately and relevantly to argue their cases – without a historian's name in sight!

What makes a good extended essay structure?

There is not much difference in structure between a good Extended Essay and a good class essay. By the time you do your Extended Essay you should know that essay writing is not just about facts but also about a structured argument. But there are points about the Extended Essay worth repeating here.

The introduction is the most vital part of any essay

Your introduction creates a first impression and it gets a marker on your side if you show that you are arguing a case, not just telling a story. Your introduction should provide a clear indication of the route you intend to take through your essay and the points you intend to develop. Once you have a good introduction the rest of the essay should flow logically from it. You should be able to use your introduction as a point-by-point paragraph guide.

This introduction to an essay on the growth of democracy shows what I mean.

EXAM EXAMPLE

Do you agree that Britain became more democratic between 1850 and 1918?

For any country to be called democratic certain conditions have to exist. First of all, adults should have the vote (1) but the right to vote itself did not make Britain democratic. Between 1850 and 1918 other features in a democracy were created. These features included a fair system of voting (2), a choice of who to vote for (3) and access to information to make an informed choice. (4) It should also be possible for adults to become MPs themselves (5) and parliament should be accountable to the voters (6). Between 1850 and 1918 most, but not all, of these conditions had been met, so Britain was more of a democracy but not entirely democratic.

> You'll see there are six numbered points here. It is entirely up to you but some students find it useful to number main ideas with a pencil. The numbers help to show how many separate development section paragraphs there should be.

After the introduction

The long middle section of your essay must develop each one of the themes, points or issues raised in your introduction.

Each new point should be a new paragraph. Each new paragraph must start with a main sentence that makes clear what the point of the paragraph will be. At the end of each paragraph try to link the point you have developed back to the main question. That sentence shows to a marker that your paragraph is relevant to the overall title and that you are doing what you have been asked to do.

After one well-structured paragraph, go on to the next. This should be based on the next point raised in your introduction. It should follow the same format advice, continuing your main argument and showing off more of your factual knowledge.

The conclusion

Your conclusion should answer the main question. It should summarise the points that support one side of the argument. It should then sum up the arguments against the idea in the title. End with your final decision.

Start by writing 'In conclusion…' and write one sentence that gives a general answer to the main question.

Then write 'On the one hand…' and summarise the information that supports one point of view about the essay title.

Then write 'On the other hand…' and here you must sum up the evidence that gives a different point of view about the main question.

Finally, write 'Overall…' and then write an answer to the main question, perhaps including what you think is the most important point made which led you to your final, overall answer.

Here is an example of a conclusion to the question 'How far did Britain become more democratic between 1867 and 1918? Remember, each of the four stages of the conclusion should only last for one sentence, so in total you have a concise four sentence conclusion.

> *In conclusion, Britain did become more democratic between 1867 and 1918 but was not yet fully a democracy.*
>
> *On the one hand more people gained the right to vote, the system became fairer, there was more choice and people had access to information to make informed choices.*
>
> *On the other hand, women did not yet have full political equality with men.*
>
> *Overall, Britain was much more democratic than it had been in 1867 but still had some way to go, including even reforming the UK 'first past the post' voting system which still raises criticisms.*

MARKING

Your essay will be marked in three sections.

- There is a maximum of 6 marks for structure.
- There is a maximum of 12 marks for knowledge.
- There is a maximum of 12 marks for analysis.

Each of the three sections has specific criteria to help the marker decide how many marks to award. (See overleaf)

How are marks awarded for structure?

You will get 1 or 2 marks if:

- You have made some attempt to organise your work into a beginning, middle and end.
- You try to set the scene by describing the background to the issue in the title.
- You try to develop your answer by including some relevant factual information.
- Your conclusion is really just a summary of points made in your essay.

You will get 3 or 4 marks if:

- You have an introduction that sets out the context.
- Your introduction includes several relevant points that you intend to develop in the essay.
- Your information is organised into paragraphs.
- Each paragraph develops a separate main point.
- Each paragraph includes a lot of relevant information that helps to explain the points you have made in your introduction.
- Your conclusion clearly sums up the points you have made and they are directly connected to the main question.

You will get 5 or 6 marks if:

- Your introduction sets the scene (context), shows clearly the line of argument you will follow and also signposts the relevant themes and ideas you will develop in your answer.
- Your development is based on well-organised paragraphs, containing accurate and relevant information. Each paragraph must make a clear point in answer to the main question.
- Your conclusion sums up the ideas you have presented and weighs up different points of view in order to reach a balanced decision linked directly to the main question.

How are marks awarded for knowledge?

● You will not get any knowledge marks within your introduction so do not waste time including factual details.

● You will score marks each time you use a correct and relevant piece of information to support a main point.

● You will get a second mark if you develop that information point further.

However, you will not get a mark for every piece of information you include. Supposing you wrote, 'The Liberals passed many social reforms, one of which was Old Age Pensions. In 1908 Lloyd George introduced the Old Age Pensions Act that provided between 1 shilling and 5 shillings a week to people over seventy. These pensions were only paid to citizens on incomes that were not over 12 shillings. The pensions were only paid to people of good character who had not been in prison for the previous ten years.'

This paragraph has at least seven hard facts in it. Clearly, it would be unfair to give 7 out of 12 knowledge marks just on pensions. So no matter how much you write on PART of your answer, you will only score at most 2 marks for knowledge.

How are marks awarded for analysis?

You will get 1 or 2 marks if:

- You mostly just tell a story with hardly any attempt to link your information to the main question.

You will get 3 or 4 marks if:

- You are still mainly telling a story but in almost every paragraph you make a comment linked to the question. For example, in a question on the effectiveness of the Liberal Reforms in helping the poor, this answer got a mark for analysis:

  'The Liberals started Old Aged Pensions to over 70 year olds but most old people did not live that long so the Liberal Reforms were only limited in their help.'

You will get 5 or 6 marks if:

- You clearly know where you are going with the essay and you USE your information to link into a comment about the question.

You will get 7 or 8 marks if:

- You are using your information to support your ideas about the issue throughout your answer.

You will get 9 or 12 marks if:

- Your answer is well developed with lots of accurate and relevant information.
- You show your awareness of different points of view about the issue you have chosen. This is called 'historiography'.

Finally…

You should now be ready to tackle your Extended Essay. Good luck! But remember that people make their own luck. Success in the Extended Essay comes from careful preparation and then putting your preparation into practice by using the 2 hours you have to show off your best possible work.

2 Higher History Paper 1

INTRODUCTION

Your exam booklet is divided into two main Historical Study sections – British History and European/World History.

What do I have to do in Paper 1?

In total you must write two essays. One essay must answer a question from the British topics. The other essay must answer a question from the European/World topics.

The British History Historical Study is divided into five study topics:

- Church, State and Feudal Society
- The Century of Revolutions 1603–1702
- The Atlantic Slave Trade
- Britain 1851–1951
- Britain and Ireland 1900–1985

You will have studied ONE of these topics. Each topic has three questions to choose from.

You must answer ONE of those questions.

The European/World Historical Study is divided into nine study topics:

- The Crusades 1071–1204
- The American Revolution 1763–1787
- The French Revolution, to 1799
- Germany 1815–1939
- Italy 1815–1939
- Russia 1881–1921
- USA 1918–1968
- Appeasement and the Road to War, to 1939
- The Cold War 1945–1989

You will have studied ONE of these topics. Each topic has three questions to choose from.

You must answer ONE of those questions.

RACE AGAINST TIME – PAPER 1

How much time do I have to complete Paper 1?

The Paper 1 examination lasts for 1 hour and 20 minutes (80 minutes). Your target is to write TWO essays in 80 minutes. Remember, that's one essay from the British History Historical Study and one from the European/World Historical Study.

Could I do two essays from the same Historical Study, especially if I don't see any questions I want to answer in the other section?

No. Never do two essays from the same Historical Study. If you do, both essays will be marked but only the essay with the best mark will be counted. The other essay will get 0 marks, no matter how good it is.

If I spend too long on the first essay should I still try to do a second essay?

YES! First of all DO NOT spend too long on one essay. You MUST be disciplined about time and spend only 40 minutes on your first essay. Otherwise, any time taken over 40 minutes is really time being stolen from your second essay.

Think about this: If you have written quite a good first essay you might get 14/20 marks after 40 minutes of writing. If you decide to write only one essay, and use all your time on it, you might push it up to 17/20. That means you have gained 3 marks by overshooting time. Unless your second essay is completely and utterly wrong, is irrelevant or only lasts a few lines you are still guaranteed to get more than 3 marks. If your second essay even slightly tries to answer the question – even if there are errors and some of it is irrelevant – you will still get about 7 or 8 marks. So, with the example here, 14 marks plus 8 equals 22 marks – and that's a pass since 20/40 is half marks.

By only doing one essay, even one that is a very good A pass, you will only get 17/40 – a poor fail.

The rule is this – organise your time and **DO TWO ESSAYS**.

THE ESSAY QUESTIONS

What will the essay questions be like?

ALL essays are a similar style. You will never get a 'tell a story' essay that asks you only to 'describe'. In the Higher History exam you will always be asked whether or not you agree with a particular point of view or you will be asked to explain something. You will find examples of typical questions on page 10.

Is there a 'must remember' rule about writing essays?

Yes. The single most important piece of advice to any candidate is 'read the question: what does it ask you to **DO**?' The SQA has reported that if candidates read each question carefully and work out what it asks them to do it would make a massive contribution to raising standards of performance. Every year markers find a significant number of essays written by candidates who seem to have a prepared answer in their heads and use it as their answer regardless of the exact wording in the real exam question. The reason for this is that candidates presumably hoped for different questions and failed to adapt their answers. Don't be one of these candidates.

What should I do first when I open my exam question booklet?

- Make yourself think. Breathe deeply. You will be nervous and adrenaline will be pumping. You will want to get started quickly but take your time.

- Make sure you are looking at the questions in the section of the course you have studied.

- Look for questions you might want to answer.

- Make sure you have understood not only what the question is about but also what you have to **do**. In other words, see what the topic is but also understand what the task is.

- Finally, read all the questions again in your chosen topic and make sure the one you have chosen gives you the best chance to score highly.

Should I write a mini plan for my essay?

Many candidates find it helpful to write a mini plan along the lines of the signpost idea mentioned elsewhere in this chapter. Briefly, a signpost simply shows where your essay is going. It makes you think about the question and what you need to do to be successful. You then need to think about what the main relevant sections in your essay should be. Once you have done that, you have the skeleton of your essay planned out. That's your signpost. You can bullet these points or draw a small spider diagram – whatever helps you get started on an organised, relevant answer to the question.

How do I make sure I answer the question properly?

Any essay question has two parts – the TOPIC and the TASK. The topic is what you will see first when you open your exam paper and look at the questions quickly. You will be asking yourself what the essays are about. Do you know information about this topic? The task is to understand what you have to DO with your information. Are you sure you understand what the question wants you to do? How do you make your information RELEVANT to the question?

Candidates who score highly in Paper 1 do so because they read the question and then answer the question asked, not the one they practised weeks or months before.

Is it enough just to write out as much information as I know?

No, it is not. Essay writing is about knowing detailed information BUT it is even more important to know the process and technique of HOW to write a good essay.

WRITING AN INTRODUCTION

Why is an introduction important?

An introduction is where your essay starts to take life – or starts to struggle. Without an introduction there will be no structure because you have not thought HOW you intend to answer the question. If your plan is not sorted out before you write your introduction, your essay might decline into storytelling – at best a C award. The introduction is where you must do your hardest thinking about the topic, what you must do and what will be the main stages of your answer. Your introduction should signpost your main ideas. It should provide you with a sequenced guide to follow through the rest of the essay.

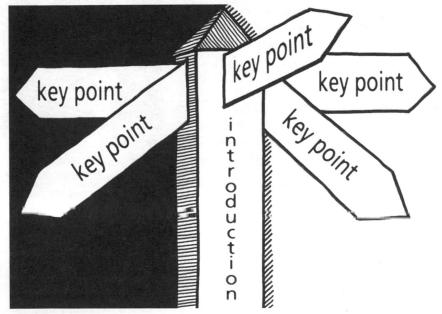

Why is an introduction important?

An essay is not just a long story containing as many names, dates and facts as you can remember. That will gain you at MOST only 6 marks out of 20. Your answer must be relevant to the question. It must also be structured with a beginning, a middle and an end.

Why must my essay have a structure?

If you don't know where you are going you will never get there. In other words, a successful essay needs a plan. That plan must help you to answer the question set. You will never get a question that states, 'Write all you know about...'. You will be asked to use information and your own thoughts to argue your case.

You could be asked whether you agree with an opinion or not.

You might be asked to explain why certain things happened.

You might be asked to judge if something was a success or a failure.

All these types of questions require you to answer in a thoughtful, structured way.

MARKING

How will my essay be marked?

When doing any piece of work that is to be assessed or marked it makes a lot of sense to know how it will be marked. Your essays will be marked in a very similar way to your Extended Essay. There will be marks for structure, knowledge and analysis.

Structure

You will gain up to 4 marks for structure. Structure means you must have a clear INTRODUCTION then a clear CONCLUSION.

When marking your essay many examiners will give a mark out of 4 for your introduction and a mark out of 4 for your conclusion. The marker will then divide by 2 to get an overall mark for structure, so if you do a better conclusion than introduction you will get the higher overall structure mark.

> ### Introduction
>
> You will be given a mark for including a clear scene-setting CONTEXT.

You will be given a mark for having a clear line of argument. In answer to the question 'How important was Bismarck to German unification', a line of argument could be as basic as writing 'Bismarck was important to German unification but there were several other factors.' That is a SIMPLE line of argument.

You will also be given a mark for including the other factors you intend to develop in your essay. For factors to develop in the essay about German unification you could write 'The other factors that were important include Prussian economic growth, the declining power of Austria, Prussia's army reforms and the growing Prussian economy thanks to the Zollverein. On top of that the 19th century saw the growth of cultural nationalism, which made people feel more German.'

The use of context, a line of argument and an indication of factors to develop will score you are least 3 marks out of 4 for your introduction.

Conclusion

Is there only a vague, short conclusion? If so, give 1 mark.

Is the conclusion just a summary of points, possibly already listed in the introduction? If so, give 2 marks.

Is the conclusion clearly linked to the question and based on evidence presented? If so, give 3 marks.

Is there a balanced conclusion, summarising the arguments in the essay and coming to an overall judgement relating to the question? If so, give 4 marks.

To write an effective conclusion, follow the model on page 42.

Knowledge

You will get up to 6 marks for accurate and relevant factual knowledge. You will score 1 mark each time you use a correct piece of information to support a main point. You will get a second mark if you develop that information point further. However, you will not get a mark for every piece of information you include. You will not get any knowledge marks within your introduction so keep to the point.

Supposing the question asked:

How important was Bismarck to the unification of Germany?

Here is part of an answer to this question:

> *'Bismarck fought three wars. The second was against Austria. He had settled the war with Denmark at the Convention of Gastein but this left Austria in a tricky position. When an argument broke out over the ruling of Holstein, Bismarck used it as an excuse to provoke a war with Austria. After a short seven-week war Austria was defeated at the Battle of Konigratz, also known as Sadowa. Prussian military tactics and technology were better and Prussian troops used the latest breech loading needle gun. Austrian casualties were high. Bismarck then arranged a quick peace settlement with Austria at the Treaty of Prague'.*

Clearly this part of the answer is just telling a story but in terms of knowledge there are at least ten hard facts in the answer. It would not be fair to give all 6 knowledge marks when there are so many other factors in German unification that have to be explained.

Analysis (or argument)

You will get up to 10 marks (half your total) for using your information to answer the question asked. You must show you have understood the question and are using your information and ideas to answer the question directly. It's never enough just to tell a story.

The following marking scheme might help you to know in what ways you get certain marks for analysis and how you could improve.

Analysis

If your essay is almost entirely storytelling (narrative) with little or no clear attempt to answer the question then you will get between 0 and 1 mark.

If your essay **just tells a story** and any comments you make are relevant to the **subject of the essay but not the exact question** you will only get 1 mark.

If you make a **comment that is relevant to the question**, after a section of narrative, you will get 2–3 marks. For example, in a question about Appeasement: 'This shows that Prime Minister Chamberlain was important in keeping Britain out of war in 1938.'

If you use **the style** of the 2–3 mark section but use it **consistently in every paragraph** between the introduction and the conclusion you will get between 4 and 5 marks.

If you make comments that show you are thinking about your information and linking it to the issue in the question you will get 6 or 7 marks. In an essay about the reasons for the growth of the Civil Rights movement in the USA, an analysis point worth 6 or 7 marks might be 'this meant that publicity was important in gaining sympathy for the campaign or more importantly in turning public opinion against white racist authority in the South'.

If you make consistent analytical comments throughout your essay you will get 8–9 marks. In an essay about the causes of the Liberal Reforms, comments such as 'This shows that the new Liberal politicians understood that it was important to target help on the deserving poor and this was a big departure from the previous laissez faire attitudes.'

Finally, for 10 marks your information should be used in a fluent, organised and sustained analysis. Your analysis should run throughout the essay and be supported by evidence rather than comments added on after a storytelling section. It is also important to show an awareness of different points of view and differing interpretations of the evidence. Remember, it is NOT vital to include historians' names or quotes – but doing so could help you. It would also help you to prioritise your arguments and weigh them up before reaching your final decision (which should relate directly to the question).

In an essay about German unification a good analytical comment could be 'There are differing views about the real reasons for unification. Some say that Bismarck was the vital catalyst in unification, but others argue that without a strong economy and a strong army Bismarck's diplomacy would not have been so successful. However, a strong argument is that Bismarck did not deal the cards but he did play his hand well to achieve unification. This can be shown by… (At this point use detailed and accurate information to support your argument.)

What is the first thing I should do before I write my introduction?

Suppose the first question you look at is this:

> To what extent did the Liberals hope to win political advantage by starting a programme of social reforms after 1906?

First of all THINK! Ask yourself what the question is about. At first, you will see the words 'Liberals', 'social reform' and '1906'. It looks like the question is about what the Liberal Reforms did – but it is not.

The essay title provides one possible explanation for why the Liberal Reforms happened, and you are asked if you agree with that view or should other reasons be considered. So the question is really about WHY the Liberal Reforms happened. You have to decide if political advantage was the real reason or if other reasons were more important.

You should know that there were other reasons apart from political advantage. This question asks 'to what extent' so you should be aware that you must show off your knowledge about the other reasons and arrive at a balanced conclusion.

Are there certain things that must be in an introduction?

Yes, it must have a sentence which suggests you are going to write a balanced essay by looking at all sides of the debate. You could do this by stating that political advantage was only one of many reasons for the reforms. Then you should mention the other reasons but do not explain them yet. Remember that this is your introduction. It should be written in a 'grown up' style avoiding the first person as in 'I think…' and it should just indicate the main points you intend to develop.

What is the difference between a poor introduction and a good one?

To answer that question it is best to use some real examples.

EXAM EXAMPLE 1

Here is a very weak introduction to an answer to the following question:

> To what extent did the Liberals hope to win political advantage by starting a programme of social reforms after 1906?

In order to answer this question it is necessary to explain why the Liberal reforms happened and decide if political advantage was a main reason. The Liberal Reforms began in 1906 and were passed to help the old, the young, the sick and the unemployed.

Why is this a very weak introduction?

It is far too short – only two sentences long. This introduction does nothing to help the writer. Time is wasted by almost writing out the question. All it does is pretend to be an introduction. There is no thought here about how the essay will develop. There is no signposting of any ideas about why the reforms happened. The second sentence is completely irrelevant. It is about the reforms, suggesting that the writer has not understood the question.

Here is a better, but still not very good introduction.

There were many reasons why the Liberal reforms were passed after 1906. Political advantage was one reason but so were the effects of reports on poverty from Rowntree and Booth. Rowntree was a York businessman and Booth was a London one and they both found out that almost 30 percent of the population in their cities lived in poverty. The Liberals were also worried about national efficiency and national security. There were also new ideas about what the Liberal Party should do to help people too poor to help themselves.

Why is this better but still not very good?

The writer understands that the question is about why the reforms were passed but the reasons are listed in a very basic way. There is extra information, developing the point about poverty reports that is not appropriate in an introduction. However, this introduction does provide a foundation to build upon.

Here is a much better introduction.

By the early 20th century most men, rich and poor, could vote. The new Labour Party promised social reform and the Liberals were worried about losing votes. A reform could therefore be seen as a rather selfish, politically advantageous response to political change. (1) The Liberal Reforms were also partly a result of concern for the poor that had been highlighted by the reports of Booth and Rowntree. (2) Other factors also played a part. The spread of municipal socialism (3) inspired some Liberals to attempt social reform on a national scale. Concerns over national efficiency and security played a part in the reforms. (4/5) Finally new attitudes in the Liberal Party, called New Liberalism, caused the Liberals to move away from the laissez-faire ideology of the 19th century. (6)

Why is this a better introduction?

It is an appropriate length. The style is mature and signposts clearly the points to be raised in the essay. There is no irrelevance and it is clear to a marker that you have understood the question.

If it helps, there is no reason why you cannot faintly number your separate points with a pencil as a guide to yourself of what the main development paragraphs should be about. It provides a structure that you could follow through the rest of the essay.

Here is another reminder about introduction techniques, this time from a question in the Appeasement and the Road to War topic.

EXAM EXAMPLE 2

> How successfully did Germany pursue its foreign policy between 1933 and March 1938?

Your introduction must outline what you will do.

This question asks 'how successfully' and you can only judge success against what Hitler wanted to achieve. In this essay, you must establish what Germany's foreign policy aims were. Once you have done that you have a structure to your essay and you can use your factual knowledge to develop the main themes.

Here is an example of an introduction that signposts where you will go.

German foreign policy between 1933 and 1938 was largely based around Hitler's aims outlined in Mein Kampf. His first aim was to destroy the terms of the Treaty of Versailles. (1) His second was to create a Greater Germany including all German-speaking peoples. (2) Another Nazi aim was to achieve Lebensraum for Germany and that was to be found in Russia and Eastern Europe. (3) Finally Nazi ideology was racist and within his foreign policy Hitler wanted to establish the power of the Aryan master race over the inferior peoples of Eastern Europe. (4)

The numbered sentences indicate the signposted points in the introduction that can be expanded into one paragraph for each point. This introduction is now ready to develop.

DEVELOPING MY ESSAY

Any essay must have a beginning, a middle and an end. This section is about the middle part that will become the longest part of your essay. It is here that you must develop or expand the points made in your introduction. That is why markers and teachers often refer to the middle part as the 'development section' of your essay.

What information should I include in the middle section?

Most of the development section of your essay will contain detailed information but beware you don't wander off into irrelevant storytelling. When you reach the end of a paragraph ask yourself, 'why have I written this section?' If you don't know why, how will a marker know? Make sure you make your material relevant by ending each paragraph with a mini conclusion linking back to the main question.

Should I try to use primary and secondary evidence in essay development?

Yes, if you can. The opinions of historians, contemporary views or statistics can all be used to support your argument but the important word here is RELEVANCE. Does the information used reinforce points you are making or are you just including such evidence as 'stand alone' information with no direct connection to the question set? If there is no connection to the main question, then you must think seriously about the inclusion of such material. Although the information you want to include is detailed and accurate, you might lose marks if it is not used in a relevant way within your essay.

What is a good and a bad development paragraph?

Here are examples of different development paragraphs from an essay from the USA topic.

EXAM EXAMPLE 3

> How far did the civil rights movement in the USA achieve success in the 1950s and 60s?

Suppose that the introduction to this essay **had already stated** that one important reason was the gaining of national publicity and that is the point the following paragraphs tries to develop.

Here is a weak development paragraph.

In 1955 Rosa Parks sat on a 'whites only' seat in Birmingham Alabama (That's a factual error. It was Montgomery, Alabama) *and refused to get up when she was asked to. Rosa was tired and was arrested. When news spread about her arrest a bus boycott started and it lasted over a year. There were also sit ins and freedom rides and a March on Washington.*

Why is this a weak paragraph?

There is no starting main sentence linking to the introduction that lets a marker know what to expect. There are factual errors. For a good mark your information must be accurate and relevant. This essay wanders into irrelevance by writing too much about Rosa Parks. It is poorly organised, bringing in other protests that are not explained. There is no clear connection between the information, the point about publicity or even the main question. In other words there is no sign of this information being used to make a point that is relevant to the main question.

Here is a much better development paragraph.

The gaining of sympathy and publicity by protests was a vital part of the success of the civil rights campaigns. When Rosa Parks refused to give up her seat on a bus in Montgomery Alabama she started a bus boycott which gained wide publicity and led to the emergence of an important leader, Martin Luther - two vital ingredients in explaining why the campaigns were successful. King's speeches were eventually shown live on national television, proving the importance of the media, especially TV news, for attracting sympathy and support.

Why is this a much better paragraph?

A strong main sentence links to the introduction and lets the marker know what to expect. There are no factual errors and the information included is relevant to the question. There is no doubt this information is being used to make a point – there is a mini conclusion linking directly to the main question. Throughout the paragraph there are several links back to the main question so the marker is quite clear why the factual information is being included in the essay.

Do I have to write a development paragraph for every main point I put in my introduction – and how do I do it?

Yes, you do and building a good development is straightforward once you have a clear introduction.

You might remember from the section on writing introductions that one tip is to remind yourself about the main points in an answer by numbering them in your introduction. That way you have thought out what the main points will be and you have organised the sequence of paragraphs in the development section and what they will be about. All you have to do is develop the ideas!

Here is an example from the Later Modern section on Britain and Scotland.

EXAM EXAMPLE 4

> Why was the right to vote given to more and more people between 1867 and 1918?

Here is a good introduction to the question.

There were many reasons why the franchise (the right to vote) was extended to more and more people in 1867, 1884 and 1918. (1) These reasons included trying to win advantages for a particular political party (2), changing attitudes towards the 'lower classes' (3) and the effect of the Great War (4) that acted as a catalyst and speeded up change.

Probably the most important reason was the effect of the Industrial Revolution (5) that changed where people lived, how they worked and how they felt about their position in society. Finally, another important reason why the franchise was extended was the change in political ideology (6) from believing the right to vote should only belong to people who owned the land of Britain to believing that the vote should be the right of all adult British citizens.

Here is the sort of information you would be expected to include in each paragraph to suitably develop your middle section.

1. This point sets the context, establishes that you know what the question is about and shows off knowledge of when the reform acts were passed. It also lets the marker know that you intend to deal with why the reforms happened (which is what the question asks) rather than write down the terms of the act, which is seldom asked about directly.

2. This is a reference to political parties adopting the ideas of other parties and attracting voters by promising changes in order to prevent the other party from winning an election. That was especially true of the circumstances around the 1867 Reform Act. The phrases 'stealing the Liberals clothes' and 'dishing the Whigs' would be appropriate here once you know what they mean!

3. Here the point should be made that by 1867 urban, skilled, working class men were educated and not revolutionary, and therefore should be admitted to the political system and granted the vote. In 1884 the same was true of other men in the countryside and in towns. If they were not allowed to vote they might turn to the new ideology of socialism that was seen as a threat. There were also views that working people as citizens of the country deserved to have a vote as the ideology of democracy gained greater acceptance in the country. Another more cynical point could be that the ordinary electorate could only cast a vote but had no political influence within parliament. They were far from the reigns of power, which were still in the hands of an educated and wealthy elite within parliament.

4. The Great War changed many attitudes. Most answers state that women gained the vote because of their war work. That is not entirely true. Most of the women who worked in the war effort were below thirty so they got no vote in 1918. Perhaps there were other reasons for extending the franchise in 1918.

    One clue could be that for one election only, right after the war, ex-servicemen who were nineteen or over gained the vote. So perhaps changes in the right to vote had more to do with the conscription of young men to fight and the realisation that, as citizens, people had the right to choose governments which may decide to send men off to kill on behalf of that government. So, maybe this point about the effect of the Great War is not as simple as first thought. After all, this reform extended the vote to all MEN over twenty-one as well as women over thirty. However, the war was certainly a catalyst for change.

5. This is an important point to make. Britain was changing very quickly after 1850. Cities were growing and social classes were emerging. Large cities and factories housed thousands of people who suffered terrible working and living conditions. If they were not 'taken into' the system by giving them the vote, would they try to overthrow the system with revolution? It was also true that other industrial countries were becoming more democratic. Political 'freedom' issues had become popular in the USA and Europe in the late 19th century. Why not in Britain also?

6. A main theme in this course is change in ideology. By 1918 there was a belief that parliament represented the people of Britain, not just the owners of land and property. A point to make could be that by 1918 the vote was considered to be a right for the many and not a privilege for the few.

Middle section checklist

To sum up, here is a checklist for the essential structure of your middle section.

- You should have an introductory sentence for each paragraph outlining what the paragraph will be about.

- You must develop one main point per paragraph.

- Each paragraph should end with a clear, relevant link back to the main question.

- Your information must be detailed, accurate and relevant.

- Your subject-specific vocabulary must be very accurate and correctly used. That means that names, ideas and events relevant to the topic must be correctly applied.

- You should make regular, clear links between the content of each paragraph and the main question.

REACHING AND WRITING CONCLUSIONS

Must I finish with a conclusion?

Your conclusion is as important as all the other sections of your essay. Unless you have a suitable conclusion you are likely to gain less than half marks. Quite simply, you must have a conclusion that ends your essay by summing up your main arguments and providing a final answer to the main question.

How do I write a good conclusion?

A conclusion should have four main stages.

- The first sentence starts with 'In conclusion' and states an overall view of the answer.
- The second stage could start 'On one hand...' in order to introduce one side of your balanced conclusion.
- The third stage starts with 'On the other hand...' and here you present some evidence that balances or counters your earlier evidence.
- Your final sentence is where you weigh up your two sides of the argument and make your overall decision, perhaps starting with 'On balance...'

Here is an example to illustrate how this would look in reality.

EXAM EXAMPLE 5

The following conclusion is to the essay title:

> To what extent did hope of gaining political advantage force the Liberals into a programme of social reform from 1906?

In conclusion, the Liberal Reforms were the result of many influences. On one hand, political advantage was an important factor in pushing the Liberals towards social reform. Fears of losing votes to the new Labour Party may have made the reforms a more pressing necessity. On the other hand. Without the reports of Booth and Rowntree making people aware of dire poverty in Britain, perhaps the Liberals would not have responded with a programme of reforms. On balance, these reports, with the example of municipal socialism, made people realise that governments could help ease the problems of poverty that were often beyond the individual's ability to help themselves.

3 Higher History Paper 2

INTRODUCTION

From 2011 onwards, Paper 2 of Higher History will be completely different from any earlier Higher History exam paper. Beware of using earlier past papers. They will not be accurate.

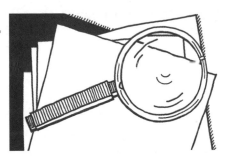

What will Higher History, Paper 2 be about?

Paper 2 will contain five different sets of questions, one set for each special topic.

There are five Scottish-based Special Topics. These topics are:

- The Wars of Independence, 1286–1328
- The Age of the Reformation, 1542–1603
- The Treaty of Union, 1689–1740
- Migration and Empire, 1830–1939
- The Impact of the Great War on Scotland, 1914–1928

Do I have to choose which special topic to answer?

No. Your teacher/tutor will have made the decision which special topic you study. Make sure you answer questions on the correct Special Topic.

What do I have to do?

You will have five sources to use and four questions to answer.

You will have 1 hour and 25 minutes to do that.

That means you will have about 15 minutes to answer a 5 mark question and about ½ hour to answer a 10 mark question, so answers must be well structured and well developed. Put simply, that means you must do three things in each answer:

- You must do what the question asks you to do.
- You must use the information provided in the source.
- You must include your own relevant, recalled knowledge.

Each question also has its own particular process that you must use to answer it successfully. Later in this chapter there are sample answers to show you how to deal with the different questions.

How do I know what the content of each Special Study topic is?

The content is what you have been learning in class. More precisely, your special topic syllabus is divided into six main issues. You can look them up yourself if you wish on the SQA website at:

http://www.sqa.org.uk/sqa/files_ccc/History_Higher_2010.pdf

Scroll down to pages 44–48 and there you will find detailed descriptions of the content of each and every topic in Paper 2. The first issue you will see in each topic is called 'Background'. The last issue is called 'Perspective'. Neither of those issues will have any questions asked about them. They are NOT examined. That leaves four other issues – and each one of those issues has a question linked to it.

What types of questions will I be asked?

There are four different types of question. Each of the four questions tests different skills such as evaluation and comparison. The rest of this chapter gives advice about how to answer the types of question you will be asked in Paper 2.

There will be a source evaluation question worth 5 marks.

This will usually be identified with a question asking 'How useful is source... as evidence of...'. In this type of question you are being asked to judge how good the source is as a piece of historical evidence.

There will be a comparison question worth 5 marks.

You will be asked to compare two points of view overall and in detail. The question MIGHT NOT use the word compare. The wording of the question could be something like ' To what extent does Source B agree with Source C about...'.

There will be a 'How far' question worth 10 marks and a 'How fully' question worth 10 marks also.

The 'How far' question is to test your knowledge of one specific part of an issue, called a sub-issue.

The 'How fully' question is to test your knowledge of a whole issue.

To find the exact structure and style of the questions you will be asked, go to: http://www.sqa.org.uk/sqa/files_ccc/History%20Higher%20Specimen%202011.pdf and scroll down to pages 5–9. There you will find information about the 'How far' / 'How fully' questions you will be asked in your special topic.

THE IMPORTANCE OF SOURCES

What are sources?

Sources are extracts of information taken from first-hand historical documents or from history books written after the events they describe. During your course of study you will have seen lots of sources, some primary, some secondary. Some of them are written, sometimes they are maps, photos, cartoons and even poems and songs. All of these sources tell you something about how people felt or what they did at the time, or what historians thought afterwards.

Why are sources referred to as primary or secondary?

A primary source is any source produced around the time of the event described or shown in the source. Primary sources can include opinions or descriptions written by people who were alive at the time but who produced the source later – such as autobiographies or memoirs based on diaries kept at the time.

People who did not experience first hand the events they comment on produce secondary sources. For example, historians writing about the Crusades were not alive hundreds of years ago. They have researched their subject, probably using primary sources to research their work on the subject.

Are primary sources better than secondary sources?

No, not always. A primary source might let you know how someone felt at the time but what if their understanding of an event or their knowledge was limited? Primary sources might also be biased.

A secondary source usually has the advantage of hindsight and research and the producer of the source is more likely to be objective and unbiased.

In short, all the sources you are given are useful in the context of the exam and it is often your task to evaluate the content and the opinions in the source.

How many sources will there be in my exam paper?

There will be five sources to use. An exam paper may have three primary sources and two secondary sources or the other way around. There will always be a 3/2 or 2/3 split.

Why are we given sources in the exam?

Sources are the raw materials of history. Historians have skills and to be successful in Higher History you are expected to be able to use these skills of analysis in reaching balanced answers to questions using the available evidence, both from the sources provided and from your own knowledge. The four different questions in Paper 2 test your skills as a historian.

RACE AGAINST TIME – PAPER 2

How many marks is Paper 2 worth?

Paper 2 is worth a total of 30 marks. Each of the four question types has its own number of marks indicated after it. Evaluation and comparison questions will be worth 5 marks each. But the 'How fully' and 'How far' questions will be worth 10 marks each.

How much time do I have to complete Paper 2?

In Paper 2, timing is vital – but plan for it and use it to your advantage. The Paper 2 examination lasts for 1 hour and 25 minutes (85 minutes) and your target is to answer all four questions in that time.

How can I make sure I give enough time to each question?

There are 30 marks' worth of questions to answer in 85 minutes so that is almost 3 minutes a mark.

If you allow 2 minutes per mark to write your answers that means you will write for 60 minutes and 25 minutes throughout the exam just to READ and THINK.

Do simple multiplication – if you have a 5 mark question you should WRITE for 10 minutes. That's one page of A4. A 10 mark question should take you about 20 minutes to write – about two pages.

Will the different styles of questions always be in the same order, year after year?

No! For example, a 'how useful' evaluation question might appear as question 1 one year then might be the last question the following year. The only thing that will stay the same is the number of marks the questions are worth.

Should I skip a question if I am unsure of the answer?

No. If you write nothing the only thing a marker can do is give you no marks. Markers will give you marks even if you have not directly answered the question. If you can select relevant extracts from the source and give a very simple answer then you might get 1 or 2 marks. Give a marker the chance to give you marks!

MARKING PAPER 2

The source evaluation question

The source evaluation question is worth 5 marks.

Firstly, you must comment on ORIGIN and PURPOSE.

You will get UP TO 2 marks for writing about the source's origin (who wrote it or where the source first appeared) and its purpose (why the source was produced).

- You will get 1 mark for identifying and commenting briefly on where the source is from and why it was produced.

- For both marks you need to explain why its origin and purpose are important in the context of the question.

Secondly, you must use INFORMATION FROM THE SOURCE.

You will get UP TO 2 marks for explaining why the parts of the source you have selected are useful in terms of the question.

- There are no marks for just copying out chunks of the source.

- Just listing relevant points from the source will gain only 1 mark.

- For both marks you must mention a point from the source and ALSO explain why the evidence you have selected is relevant to the question.

Thirdly, you must use YOUR OWN KNOWLEDGE.

You will get UP TO 2 marks for using your own detailed knowledge as long as it is relevant to the question. This is called using relevant recall.

Finally, it is helpful to MAKE SURE YOU HAVE REALLY EVALUATED THE SOURCE!

- You might, for example, want to consider whether the source is entirely useful. A source will seldom be entirely valuable or useful. It will have limitations and it's up to you to explain these limits. A useful word to use is 'partly'. You can give evidence to show that the source has its uses but also include information to suggest that the source does not give the whole picture.

By counting up the sections and marks for this question it looks like the total comes to 6 but there are 5 marks available.

Stop to think how this helps you.

If you had a weak section on origin and purpose you might only get one mark. But if your other two sections (on the content of the source and your own recall) are done well and you gain 2 marks for each part then you can still achieve the maximum 5 marks.

Here is some information about how to answer this type of question. You can get up to 2 marks for origin and purpose. You could write this:

'The source is from / by... and this makes it useful because...'

'The purpose of the source is probably to... and this makes it useful because...'

There are up to 2 marks for explaining why parts of the source identified are useful in terms of the question. Here's how you might do it:

'The source states "..." and this makes is useful to the question because...'

Do this TWICE, one for each source extract you use.

The comparison question

The comparison question is worth 5 marks.

Firstly, you must make AN OVERALL COMPARISON.

- You will get up to 2 marks for stating the main ideas or points of view in the two sources. You must also make an overall statement about the extent of the agreement or disagreement.

Secondly, you must compare the sources IN DETAIL.

- You can get UP TO 4 marks so you must try to find four different comparisons.

- You MUST show you understand the points made in the sources and explain in what ways they differ from each other or support each other.

- You must also refer explicitly to the sources, perhaps by quoting briefly, to support your comments about where the sources agree or disagree.

- It is NOT ENOUGH just to list points of difference between the sources. In fact, you might get NO MARKS for simply stating 'Source A says... but B says...'.

Thirdly, you must use your own knowledge.

- Use your own detailed knowledge to explain and support some of the points you are making.

Here is some information about how to answer this type of question:

'Overall, the sources agree about... and... and...'

'In detail, the first thing they agree about is...'
'The evidence from the first source to support this is...'
'The evidence from the second source is...'

'The second thing they agree about is...'
'The evidence from the first source to support this is...'
'The evidence from the second source is...'

'The third thing they agree about is...'
'The evidence from the first source to support this is...'
'The evidence from the second source is...'

'The fourth thing they agree about is...'
'The evidence from the first source to support this is...'
'The evidence from the second source is...'

The 'How far' question

The 'How far' question is worth 10 marks.

Firstly, you must use the source provided.

- You can get up to 4 marks for identifying relevant points in the source and explaining them.

Secondly, you must include your own accurate and relevant knowledge.

- You can get up to 7 marks for including accurate and relevant information from your own knowledge.

- Make sure the information you are including helps to answer the question and helps to reach a balanced answer.

The 'How fully' question

The 'How fully' question is worth 10 marks.

Firstly, you must use the source provided.

- You can get up to 4 marks for identifying relevant points in the source and explaining them.

Secondly, you must include your own accurate and relevant knowledge.

- You can get up to 7 marks for including accurate and relevant information from your own knowledge.

The process is the same for both types of questions so you could write your answers like this: 'The source partly explains (whatever the question is asking you about)

Firstly, the source says "…" and this is relevant to the question because…

Secondly, the source says "…" and this is relevant to the question because…

Thirdly, the source says "…" and this is relevant to the question because…

Finally, the source says "…" and this is relevant to the question because…'

You must also include 7 relevant recall points. You may have got recall marks from developing your selections from the source but you must have a fairly big recall section in each answer. Use this style: 'There are also points relevant to the question not mentioned in the source. Firstly… Secondly… etc.'

Try to do 7! But do not list.

Use accurate detail but ensure your answer makes clear how information helps to answer the question.

Now practice your skills!

Look at the following examples to see how to answer evaluation questions.

THE SOURCE EVALUATION QUESTION – PART 1

The evaluation question comes with some helpful advice. Usually it states 'In reaching a conclusion you should refer to the origins and possible purpose of the source, the content of the source and recalled knowledge.' However it might be easier and more helpful to base your answers around certain questions you should ask about a source as you evaluate it. The most straightforward are:

- WHO produced the source? In what way is that relevant to assessing the value of a source?

- WHAT the is source and how is that relevant to the question?

- WHEN was the source produced and how might that information assist the evaluation of the source?

- WHY was the source produced? What were the motives of the producer of the source?

Here is an example of a source evaluation question from The Impact of the Great War on Scotland, 1914–1928.

EXAM EXAMPLE 1

Source A: from a letter written by Private Douglas Hepburn of the London Scottish Regiment to his parents in October 1915.

> *My dear Mum and Dad,*
>
> *We have been in the trenches for ten days and had a very rough time of it coming out with only 160 men left in our battalion. The Germans at the point where we attacked were ready and too strong for us. As we rushed up to the edge the machine gun was turned on us and we suffered high casualties.*
>
> *In the morning we came back and the sight of the field was rotten. To see stretcher-bearers going here and there, doing their work and the wounded crying for the bearers was a sight that could not easily be forgotten on that grey, misty and damp morning.*

> How useful is Source A as evidence of the experience of Scottish soldiers on the Western Front?

Here is a weak answer.

The source is useful because it gives a description of a trench battle. It says they have lost a lot of men - 'coming out with only 160 men in our battalion.' It shows how the Germans were strong 'The Germans at the point where we attacked were ready and too strong for us'. The source is useful because it shows that soldiers were upset by all the deaths - ' It was a sight that could not easily be forgotten'.

Why is this a weak answer?

This answer is weak mainly because it:

- fails to evaluate by referring to the origins and possible purpose of the source;
- just describes the source;
- is useful in the detail it gives of trench warfare but mainly it just copies phrases from the source;
- contains no recalled knowledge;
- does not attempt to provide a balanced answer suggesting the source might have its limits as a totally useful piece of evidence.

How many marks is this answer worth?

There is no attempt to deal with origin or purpose – 0 marks.

It selects some relevant information from the source. However it just lists some relevant points from the source. It does not explain why the evidence selected is relevant to the question – 1 mark.

There is no recall – 0 marks.

Total marks: 1 out of 5.

Here is a much better answer.

This source is partly useful for finding out about the experiences of Scottish soldiers on the Western Front but it has limits. The source is from a soldier on the Western front so is an eyewitness who experienced what he describes. The purpose is to let his parents know how he is getting on and what his experiences are like.

This makes the source very useful as primary evidence giving first-hand detail. As it is a letter to his parents the writer is likely to tell the truth but maybe not details that would worry his parents. Letters were often censored but, from its detail, this one seems to have got past the censor.

The detail given matches up with what I know. In trench warfare defence was usually stronger than the attackers and barbed wire and machine guns usually caused the high casualties mentioned in the source.

The source mentions the stronger German position and that was also usually true. The Germans chose to dig trenches on slightly higher ground where they could see an attack coming.

The source does however have limits. It gives no information about trench life such as the lice, the food, the boredom or the fear. There is also information missing about battles such as heavy artillery barrages and even gas.

Overall the source is quite useful for giving an impression but many more letters would be needed to gain a full picture of the experience of Scottish soldiers on the Western Front.

Why is this a much better answer?

It is a better answer because it:

- not only identifies the origin and purpose of the source but also explains why each of these make it a useful source; **(2 marks)**

- provides detail of trench warfare that matches other reports and it does make clear how the evidence selected is relevant to the question; **(2 marks)**

- includes detailed recalled information. It also provides a balanced evaluation of the usefulness of the source and includes more recall that helps evaluate the evidence in terms of the question asked. **(2 marks)**

How many marks is this answer worth?

This answer scores highly simply by following the three-stage marking scheme process. The maximum number of marks for a type one question is 5 so even if this answer dropped a mark in a section, the writer would still gain full marks: 5 out of 5.

EXAM EXAMPLE 2

Here is an example of a source evaluation question from The Wars of Independence, 1286–1328.

> How useful is Source D in showing the importance of William Wallace to Scottish resistance against the English? **(5 marks)**

Source D: letter from Andrew Moray and William Wallace to the merchants of Lubeck, written in October 1297

> *Andrew of Moray and William Wallace, leaders of the army of the Kingdom of Scotland, and of the community of the realm, to their wise and discreet beloved friends the mayors and common people of Lubeck and of Hamburg, greeting and increasing sincere affection.*
>
> *We have been told by trustworthy merchants of the Kingdom of Scotland that you are considerate, helpful and well disposed in all cases and matters affecting us and our merchants and we are therefore more obliged to give you our thanks and a worthy repayment: to this end we willingly enter into an undertaking with you, asking you to have it announced to your merchants that they can have safe access to all ports of the Scottish Kingdom with their merchandise, because the Kingdom of Scotland, thanks be to God, has been recovered by war from the power of the English.*
>
> *Fare well.*
>
> *Given at Haddington in Scotland, 11 October 1297.*

Here is a weak answer.

William Wallace was important because he was a leader of Scotland who defeated the English. He fought with Andrew Moray who was another leader. The letter is useful because it shows that Wallace wants Scotland to trade with Lubeck and Hamburg to help Scotland recover from the wars with England. The letter also shows that Wallace thinks that Scotland has been freed from the English.

Why is this a weak answer?

- It has a factually weak beginning. It claims Wallace was a leader of Scotland but the letter only claims that Wallace and Moray were leaders of the army of Scotland.
- This answer outlines the very basic outline of the letter.
- There is no attempt to evaluate the origin and purpose of the letter.
- There is almost no recall or development of any point raised in the letter.

Here is a better answer.

This letter is useful as one of the few pieces of primary evidence we have about Wallace. The letter was written after the Battle of Stirling Bridge and is an attempt to tell important trading partners that Scotland was 'open for business' after 'being recovered by war from the power of the English.' Scotland needed to trade and assure foreign traders they were safe in Scotland. Many traders had been hurt by Edward's invasion of Scotland, especially the destruction of Berwick.

The letter is also important in that it shows Wallace sharing leadership of the army with Andrew Moray. It also refers to the Community of the Realm. After Stirling Bridge Wallace was made Guardian of Scotland by the Community of the Realm and in that role Wallace was trying to build up Scotland's strength. The Community of the Realm were the important church men and nobles of Scotland and their recognition of Wallace as Guardian shows his importance in resisting the English.

Lubeck and Hamburg were important north German trading partners and Scotland needed resources such as timber from there. The letter is also very diplomatic and is trying to make friends with the German merchants by calling them, 'considerate, helpful and well disposed'.

How many marks is this answer worth?

The answer deals with the origin and purpose of the letter well and makes four good points, although a marker would have to find those points scattered throughout the answer. Unlike many answers, the origin and purpose are not dealt with in one block at the beginning of the answer. This answer gets the full 2 marks for origin and purpose.

The answer develops at least four points from the source and explains their significance. This would get 2 marks.

There are at least four main pieces of recall used to develop the answer. This would get 2 marks.

So in total this answer gets full marks – 5 out of 5.

Must I always evaluate using my own knowledge as well as the source?

Yes! In this sort of question recalled knowledge is vital. For example, it is impossible to judge the usefulness of a source about the experience of Scottish soldiers on the Western Front without knowing what conditions on the Western Front were like.

THE COMPARISON QUESTION

You will always get a question in your Paper 2 exam that asks you to compare sources. It will be worth 5 marks.

A comparison question requires you to make clear connections between sources. The skill being assessed is your ability to compare and that does not mean your ability to describe two sources. You must be able to show the similarities and differences between the sources. Look at this example to see what I mean.

Your question here is to compare girl A with girl B.

A weak answer would be to describe each girl in turn.

Girl A has long blonde hair. She is skinny. She has a light coloured top on and a short skirt. She has matching shoes and is tall.

Girl B has dark curly hair. She is plump. She has a dark top on and baggy trousers. She is not very tall.

Why is this a weak answer?

Because the candidate does not demonstrate the skill of comparing. What is written here is a correct description of the two girls but at no point is there any comparison.

A much better answer would be like this.

Overall, A and B are quite different although there is one similarity. They both seem to be girls.

In detail, girl A has long blonde hair but girl B has dark curly hair. Girl A is much skinnier than girl B. The clothes they wear are also different. A is wearing a light-coloured top with a short skirt and matching shoes whereas B has on a dark top and baggy trousers which hide her footwear.

Why is this a much better answer?

In this answer there are FOUR points of detailed comparison – hair, body shape, clothes and shoes. You will also notice there is an overall comparison in that the answer identifies one similarity – they are both girls. This is exactly what the exam requires you to do. In your exam the comparison question will have as part of its 'helpful hint' the following phrase – 'Compare the content overall and in detail.'

How do I spot a comparison question?

As mentioned earlier, the comparison question MIGHT NOT use the word 'compare'. Instead, the question could ask 'To what extent does Source A agree with Source B about…'. Another easy way to spot the comparison question is that it is the only question that will refer to TWO sources.

Should I organise my answer around the words 'overall' and 'in detail'?

Yes, make it easy for a marker to give you marks by following the recommended style of answering. Start your answer with the word 'overall' and then identify the main point of agreement or disagreement in the source. You should then use the phrase 'In detail' and then write the rest of your answer comparing the sources point by point.

Take one point from the source and show how it is supported or disagreed with by the other source. Keep going to and fro between the sources until you have finished comparing them. Remember it is not enough just to quote a sentence from one source then compare by quoting from another. By all means do that as part of your answer but you should also explain the point being made in your extracts in your own words and use recall to develop your comparisons. That is what is meant by a developed comparison.

Now it's time to try some real comparison questions.

EXAM EXAMPLE 3

Exam example 3 is from Special Topic option Migration and Empire, 1830–1939.

> To what extent do Sources B and C agree about the provision of education for Irish immigrants to Scotland? Compare the content overall.   (5 marks)

Source B: from the Report of the Education Commission (Scotland) (1866)

The people in the Clyde district are of the poorest classes and this district has a large mixture of Irish immigrants. For this large Irish element and their needs there exists no school within the district, beyond a private adventure school in one of the wynds. Roman Catholic children are indeed to be found in the other schools but in comparatively small numbers and their attendance is extremely irregular. It is a fact that many children in the Clyde district, both Catholic and Protestant, but chiefly the former, attend no school.

What are these neglected children doing then, if they are selling matches and running errands, cared for by no-one, not at school? They are idling in the streets and wynds, tumbling about in the gutters.

Source C: from People and Society in Scotland Vol. II, 1830-1914 (1990), edited by W. Hamish Fraser and R. J. Morris

The largest number of schools, pupils and teachers was to be found in Glasgow, but many of those were Catholic schools outside the state system. Irish settlement, especially after the Famine, produced an ever-growing demand for Catholic schools and teachers. Nonetheless, by the 1860s, the Catholic clergy could boast that they had overcome the immense difficulties and could offer pupils instruction in the three Rs and the Bible. But the community lacked the resources to pay adequate school fees or to raise the necessary funds towards teachers' salaries and school buildings. As a result, by the end of the century, there was a growing crisis in Catholic education.

Here is a weak answer.

Source B and C agree to an extent. Source B says there was very little education for Irish immigrants but Source C says there was some but not enough. Source C says the Catholic priests did what they could to teach children reading and writing and the Bible. Source B says that not many Catholic children went to school but C says there were not enough Catholic schools to meet demand. Finally, Source B thinks that Catholic children did not want to go to school but Source C thinks there were just not enough schools to meet demand.

Why is this a weak answer?

There is only a very vague attempt to introduce the answer with an overall comparison. The writer simply picks out points from the sources and does not use any recall to explain or develop these points.

How many marks is this answer worth?

Given that the marking instructions are very clear, this answer would score few marks. It might get 1 mark for the overall comparison and 1 mark for identifying direct points of comparison. There is no recall so it cannot pass. It will get 2 out of 5 at most.

Here is a much better answer.

Overall, Source B suggests that the provision of education for Irish immigrants was almost non-existent and immigrant children did not want to attend schools. On the other hand, Source C suggests that there were not enough teachers to meet the demand for a Catholic education.

In detail, Source B states there was a lack of educational provision for Irish immigrants in the Clyde area. From 1840 onwards, huge numbers of Irish migrants arrived in the west of Scotland. The Clyde area had few resources to cope with the huge increase in demand for schools. ('For this large Irish element and their needs there exists no school within the district'.) Source C on the other hand provides a more positive view about educational provision for Catholic Irish immigrants.

The Catholic Church made big efforts to look after the Irish migrants and 'could offer pupils instruction in the three Rs and the Bible'. Partly, the church wanted to prevent assimilation with Protestant Scotland but the Church also genuinely wanted to support the immigrants.

Source B says that 'Roman Catholic children are to be found in the other schools but in small numbers' but Source C claims that demand was high for education by writing 'Irish settlement produced an ever-growing demand for Catholic schools and teachers'. In some places Catholic Irish children were not welcomed in Church of Scotland schools. Also many Catholic families did not want their children going outside their Catholic world.

Finally Source B implies that Catholic children did not want education whereas Source C suggests that the problem lay with the lack of 'resources to pay adequate school fees or to raise the necessary funds towards teachers' salaries and school buildings'. Not until the 20th century did the state provide funds for basic education for all.

Why is this a good answer?

The answer starts with an overall comparison that shows understanding of both sources so this gains 2 marks. The answer then gives at least four detailed comparisons and the comparisons are relevant and connected to each other. Recall is used to explain attitudes or details mentioned in the extracts. The answer contains comparisons of opinion but provides reasons for the differences.

How many marks is this answer worth?

This answer scored highly simply by following the marking scheme process and gains 5 out of 5. Your answer does not need to be exactly like this but there are 5 marks so you MUST try to get one overall and four direct developed comparisons.

EXAM EXAMPLE 4

This example is from Special Topic option The Impact of the Great War, 1914–1928.

> To what extent do Sources B and C agree about the supply of food during the Great War? Compare the content overall and in detail.

Source B: from an interview made in 1975 with Charlie Davies, a Scot who lived in London during the First World War

> *When I came back after the war my family told me how bad it had been. You see, us being an island hardly any food could get through because German U-boats were sinking our food convoys. My family lived on bones from the butcher made into soups. And stale bread.*
>
> *When some food did get delivered to the shops everyone for miles around crowded round the place. The queues stretched for miles, and if you were old or unsteady on your feet you stood no chance. Many, especially children, died of starvation. Food riots were very common.*

Source C: from the War Memoirs of David Lloyd George,
Prime Minister during the First World War

> *So far as the vast bulk of the population was
> concerned, this rationing system, ensured a regular
> and sufficient food supply. Although there was a
> degree of scarcity, we were never faced with famine
> or actual privation. The steady improvement in our
> national health figures during and after the war shows
> that compulsory temperance in eating was in general
> more beneficial than harmful in its effects. Credit is
> due to our people for the loyal manner in which they
> submitted themselves to these strange and unwelcome
> restrictions. Without general goodwill it would have
> been impossible to make the regulations effective.*

Here is a weak answer.

> *The two sources are about food supply in the war. One thinks
> the supply was bad. It says 'Food riots were very common'.
> The other says he thinks it is good. It says 'this rationing
> system ensured a regular and sufficient food supply'. One
> said 'Many, especially children, died of starvation' and
> the other one says, 'Credit is due to our people for the loyal
> manner in which they submitted themselves to these strange
> and unwelcome restrictions'. The sources are both about
> food supply but they say different things.*

Why is this a weak answer?

- There is no attempt to introduce the answer with an overall comparison.
- The writer does not identify what sources are being used at any time.
- The writer simply writes extracts from the sources and barely explains the point or meaning.
- Two extracts written from the sources are not about the same things so a direct comparison cannot be made.
- There are only two points that MIGHT be considered as comparisons.

At MOST this answer would get 2 marks out of 5.

Here is a much better answer.

Overall, Source B believes food shortages caused big problems whereas Source C claims the food supplies were controlled and organised so everyone had enough to eat.

Both sources may not be entirely accurate. Charlie Davies was reporting stories he had been told which might be exaggerated. Lloyd George is writing his Memoirs and they are always meant to make the writer look good so naturally rationing is described as a success.

In detail, Charlie Davies reports that hardly any food could get through whereas Lloyd George states there was a regular and sufficient food supply.

Davies refers to the unrestricted U-boat campaign of 1917 when all ships to Britain were targets. At that time, the Government introduced food rationing.

Davies claims 'Many, especially children, died of starvation' while Lloyd George states 'we were never faced with famine or actual privation'. It is possible that Davies is exaggerating since he only heard those stories when he came back from the war. On the other hand, rationing was the idea of Lloyd George, the Prime Minister, so he says that rationing was effective.

As food supplies became scarcer, prices started to rise. Rationing was an attempt to make sure people got a fair share. Davies claims his family only lived on 'bones ... and stale bread' but Lloyd George states rationing was 'in general more beneficial than harmful in its effects'. Davies also says, 'When some food did get delivered to the shops... the queues stretched for miles' and he says, 'Food riots were very common.' On the other hand Lloyd George says, 'the rationing system ensured a regular food supply'. Overall food rationing made sure everyone got a fair share of food rather than using the black market and paying high prices..

Why is this a good answer?

The answer starts with an overall comparison that shows understanding of both sources so this gains two marks. The answer then gives at least four direct comparisons that are relevant and connected to each other. The comparisons are identified by the author's name. Recall is used to explain attitudes or details mentioned in the extracts. The answer contains comparisons of opinion but provides reasons for the differences.

This answer gains 5 out of 5. This answer scored highly simply by following the marking scheme process.

A Final Tip

It is POSSIBLE that a question might ask ' To what extent do sources X and Y agree about...' and it MIGHT BE that they do not agree completely or disagree completely. Usually in a comparison question you can gain marks for identifying and explaining points where the sources agree AND ALSO where they disagree, however, sometimes you will find that the two sources do either agree completely or disagree completely. So don't always assume there will be a neat and balanced answer. Use your judgement.

THE 'HOW FAR' QUESTION – PART 2

Remember, there are four issues within each Special Topic. Each issue is divided into separate parts called 'descriptors' in the syllabus. A 'How far' is based around one of those descriptors and wants to find out how much you know on the subject.

How can I recognise this sort of question?

Usually the question will contain phrases such as 'How far does Source...?' or 'To what extent does Source...?'

Here is a selection of types of questions, one from each of the five special topics.

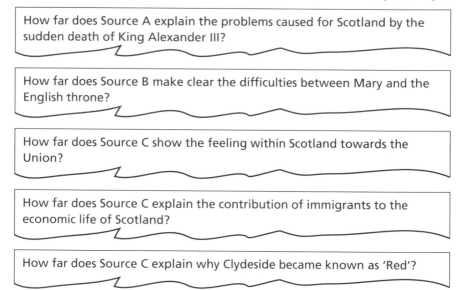

How far does Source A explain the problems caused for Scotland by the sudden death of King Alexander III?

How far does Source B make clear the difficulties between Mary and the English throne?

How far does Source C show the feeling within Scotland towards the Union?

How far does Source C explain the contribution of immigrants to the economic life of Scotland?

How far does Source C explain why Clydeside became known as 'Red'?

How do I write a good 'How far' answer?

The secret of success is to write a **balanced** answer.

First of all, you must spot relevant information in the source, quote from it briefly to help answer the question, and explain what your selection of words from the source means. Try to explain the point of view of the author of the source.

Secondly, throughout your answer you must use your own knowledge. The sources will never tell the full story so you are expected to use recall to develop your answer further. In all evaluation questions you MUST use recalled information to add relevant points or explanations to support and explain your answer.

Finally, use the word 'partly'. By writing that a source partly explains something, you are opening up the question to lead towards a balanced conclusion and also the opportunity to show off recall. By saying you agree **partly**, or a source explains something **partly**, or a source is **partly** useful, you have the opportunity to explain what the points made in the source mean, and also to explain how the source has limitations.

Can I see a simple example of how to do this type of question?

Yes. First of all, look at the drawing of the desk and then read what might seem at first to be a silly question:

How far can it be said that this desk is grey?

Clearly, the desk shown is meant to represent any source you might be given. It's also clear that the desk is not entirely grey so you cannot answer with a simple 'yes'. Equally clearly, some of the desk IS grey so you cannot answer with a simple 'no'. In other words, each source you evaluate will have some correct or useful information in it so you cannot dismiss it as useless. But equally, the source will not have all the information required so you cannot just accept the source as fully useful. The answer lies in the word **partly**.

Here is a good answer.

The desk is, I agree, <u>partly</u> grey. This is shown by the top surface that is indeed grey. On the other hand, the desk is not entirely grey – for example, there are black edges and legs that prove that the desk is not entirely grey. On the underside of the desk there is a checkerboard pattern of black and white and there are things stuck to the desk of varying colours but not identified! For these reasons, I only partly accept the description of the desk as grey.

Why is this a good answer?

This answer deals with the point of the question, recognises that much of the desk is grey, and details which parts are that colour. The answer is then balanced by identifying parts of the desk that are not grey and defines what shades and colours also exist on the desk. Finally, the answer reaches a balanced, considered conclusion that links back to the original question.

Is there a detailed process I can follow to write a good evaluation answer?

Yes. There is a simple process you can follow in the evaluation questions that can be used as a basis for a very high scoring answer. Here is how to do it.

- Read the question. What is it about? In other words, what is the subject or topic? That will then allow you to write the context setter.
- Set the context by explaining briefly the background to the events mentioned in the source. That should take NO MORE than two sentences.
- Then move on to dealing with the source. You could write, 'The first point made by the source is…' Then write 'This means…' and explain what point is being made by the extract you have selected. This is called developing the point.
- Once you have developed the point, move on to the second point in the source and repeat the process.
- Once you have finished developing the points in the source you must make sure you include recall. You could write something like 'On the other hand, the source does not cover all the points relevant at the time. For example, it does not deal with…'. That gives you a chance to show off your knowledge by explaining relevant points omitted from the source. But please remember the word relevant. Don't try to include everything you know about a topic.
- Finally, watch your time. As the question is only worth 5 marks you should only be writing for about 10 minutes.

Now have a look at this real 'How far...' question.

EXAM EXAMPLE 5

Example 5 is from the Special Topic option Migration and Empire, 1830–1939.

> How far does this source show the general opinion about the contribution of Scots to the economic growth and development of the Empire? Use the source and recalled knowledge part of the question.

Source D: from a report by the Immigration Agent for Victoria, Australia, 1853

> *I do not consider that the inhabitants of the islands of Scotland are well suited to the wants and needs of this colony. Their total ignorance of the English language makes it difficult to get employment for them while their laziness and extremely filthy habits have not made a good impression on the British people already here. It would be better if such immigration was restricted at least since these wretches have little to offer this society. Indeed, it cannot be argued other than their arrival is having a most unwelcome and detrimental effect on the inhabitants of this colony.*

Here is a weak answer.

This source does not show the general opinion about Scots abroad. Scots were mostly welcomed and played an important part in the development of the Empire. This source says Scots did not speak English but most did. Many Scots opened up the new lands so were not lazy. In many parts of the Empire Scots explored and built cities, many with Scottish names and Scottish customs which are still followed in America and Australia today. Overall, this source might just refer to some Gaelic-speaking Highlanders but even they learned new skills and worked hard.

Why is it a weak answer and how many marks is it worth?

- It is far too short. This is a 10 mark question with 4 marks possible for source analysis and 7 for recall.

- It makes simple comments about the meaning of the source and tries to argue against the opinion. However it lacks much comment on the meaning of the source so might only gain 1 out of 4 marks for this part of the answer.

- Although there are 7 marks for recall, this answer only includes two main pieces used to develop the answer. So 2 marks out of a possible 7 here.

Total marks: 3 out of 10.

Here is a better answer.

This opinion expressed in the source is the opposite of most other reports. Far from being lazy and ignorant because they could not speak English, most Scots made a vital contribution to the development of the Empire.

Scots had a reputation as good workers and despite the opinion in Source C, most Scots could read and write and spoke English. At first, Scottish soldiers and explorers opened up the new colonies and defended settlers. Many immigrant Scots were determined to succeed and they adapted well to harsh climates and difficult lands which they had experienced at home. Many Scots who emigrated were farmers who could use their knowledge of new farming methods and skills to create profitable farms. In Australia and New Zealand, Scots were important in the development of sheep farming.

Other Scots were skilled tradesmen who were needed in America, Canada, Australia, and New Zealand. Scots who were doctors, lawyers, engineers, accountants or architects were also in high demand.

Overall this report does not show the general opinion about Scots and the Empire. Even today Scots such as Andrew Carnegie and John Muir are remembered as important in the development of the Empire.

Why is this a better answer and how many marks is it worth?

- It is a much more appropriate length for a 10 mark question.

- It selects information from the source and comments on it, although this could have been developed more with other views on the contribution of Scots to the Empire. This part of the answer might gain half marks – 2 out of 4.

- This answer provides a lot of relevant, accurate recall to counter the opinion in the source.

- Recalled knowledge is used throughout the answer to provide a direct balance to the source opinion. This should gain at least 5 or 6 out of 7 for this part of the answer.

Total marks 7 or 8 out of 10.

EXAM EXAMPLE 6

This example is from the Special Topic option Scotland and the Impact of the Great War, 1914–1928.

> How far does Source D give evidence of post-war economic change and difficulties facing the Scottish economy? Use the source and recalled knowledge part of the question. **(10 marks)**

Source D: from Scottish Journey by Edwin Muir, published in 1935

> *By the late 1920s, the Clyde was launching merely 56,000 tons of shipping, and the coal industry was finding work for only 80,000 hands and producing a third less coal than in 1913. The Dundee jute trade was deeply depressed and the Borders woollen industry for the greater part of the year was on part-time working. The output of Scottish farming was falling while it was still rising in England, and in the fishing industry the numbers of those employed and the value of the catch were both steadily dropping.*

Here is a weak answer.

The source gives quite good evidence of post-war economic change and difficulty. It says 'the Clyde was launching merely 56,000 tons of shipping' which shows the shipbuilding industry was in decline. The source says 'the coal industry was finding work for only 80,000 hands and producing a third less coal than in 1913'. This means less coal was produced. It says, 'the woollen industry for the greater part of the year was on part-time working'. That means that as demand for woollen products fell the factories did not produce so much. The result was that workers were not needed 'full time' so they only got work for part of the week. As a result their wages fell. It says 'The output of Scottish farming was falling' but then says English farms were doing better. It also says the fishing industry was in difficulties so less people were employed.

Why is this a weak answer?

This answer is weak mainly because:

- It relies almost entirely on the information provided in the source.
- There is very little detailed, recalled knowledge used to develop the points.
- There is no mention of any other areas of the economy facing change or difficulties and that would be necessary in this sort of evaluation question. In other words, the candidate ignores the 'How far' part of the question.
- The candidate only uses the source and makes the most limited development points so he/she will only gain at most 2 out of 4 marks.
- There is no recall in terms of the question to provide any balance so this candidate gets 0 out of 7.

Total marks: 2 out of 10.

Here is a much better answer.

The source partly gives good evidence of post-war economic change and difficulty. It says 'the Clyde was launching merely 56,000 tons of shipping'. The use of 'merely' suggests Clyde shipbuilding was in decline. After the war, international trade fell and so did demand for ships. The war had artificially boosted the industry but, as orders dried up, production fell.

The source mentions falling numbers of workers in the coal industry. New fuels, foreign competition and the lack of investment by owners made the coal industry decline.

Scottish farming also faced difficulties. New technology benefitted larger farms but in Scotland the lack of good arable land made farming difficult.

The Scottish fishing industry was hit by war and revolution. Much of Scotland's herring catch was exported to Germany and Russia but during the war those markets were lost. The Russian revolution closed off exports to central Europe after the war. Fishing boats had been taken over by the navy and were in need of repair and replacement.

The jute industry also faced foreign competition and loss of export markets. New factories near Calcutta and also the Far East took away Dundee's trade.

Scotland's staple industries were all interlinked. Iron and steel used coal and depended on demand from shipbuilding to use the iron and steel. As shipbuilding declined with world trade so did the other connected industries. Talent in Scotland also left through emigration, sometimes to England or abroad. In the Highlands, the land question meant that farms remained relatively unproductive and inefficient. Overall, the source gives a good impression of an economy in decline and also gives reasons for many of the problems.

Why is this a much better answer?

It is a better answer because:

- It selects information from the source and uses recalled knowledge to develop each point made.
- It provides a balance to the answer by using a lot of recall about other industries and other parts of the economy.
- It ends with a short conclusion that shows the candidate has understood the question and thought about its meaning.

This answer scores highly simply by following the marking scheme process. The candidate uses the source and develops the points well, so gains 4 out of 4 marks. There is a lot of recall and most of it is relevant. Sometimes the explanations are weak such as with farming and the Highlands but overall this answer should get at least 5 out of 7 marks.

Total: 9 out of 10 marks.

THE 'HOW FULLY' QUESTION

This is the question that asks about one of the four main issues with the Special Study topic.

Once again, a useful way to start an answer to this type of question is to say 'partly'. That gives a basic answer to the question, 'How fully...'. The source will provide relevant information but will not give the whole picture. That allows you to include other information relevant to the answer from your own knowledge in order to provide a full answer.

There are two phases to any answer to this type of question.

- Firstly, you must select relevant points from the source and develop each point with recalled detailed knowledge. There are 4 marks available for doing this.

- Secondly, you must bring in your own knowledge to show there are other points relevant to the answer that are not in the sources. This part is worth up to 7 marks.

EXAM EXAMPLE 7

Example 7 is from Special Topic option The Wars of Independence, 1286–1328.

> How fully does Source D explain the relationship between John Balliol and Edward I? Use the source and recalled knowledge part of the question.

Source E: from a letter issued by King John at Kincardine or Brechin, July 1296

> *John, by the grace of God king of Scotland, greets all who shall see or hear this letter. In view of the fact that through bad and wrong advice and our own foolishness we have in many ways gravely displeased and angered our lord Edward by the grace of God king of England, in that while we still owed him fealty and homage we made an alliance with the King of France against him... we have defied our lord the king of England and have*

withdrawn ourselves from his homage and fealty by renouncing our homage... we have sent our men into his land of England to burn, loot, murder and commit other wrongs and have fortified the land of Scotland against him... for all these reasons the King of England entered the realm of Scotland and conquered it by force despite the army we sent against him, something he had a right to do as lord of his fee.

Therefore acting of our own free will we have surrendered the land of Scotland and all its people with the homage of them all to him.

Here is a weak answer to the question.

When this source was written Scotland was at war with England. Balliol was Scottish king and he had promised to be loyal to Edward. This was called 'fealty' and Balliol had done homage for the throne of Scotland. Balliol had promised to support Edward but had broken his promise by signing an alliance with France against Edward of England. This source shows that the Scots had angered Edward by attacking England and Edward had invaded Scotland. The Scots were defeated at Dunbar and Edward chased Balliol across Scotland. This source shows that Balliol and the Scots have surrendered to Edward. The relationship between Balliol and Edward is that Balliol is now defeated and in danger of losing his crown.

Why is this a weak answer?

The answer really only describes what is in the source. There is only a vague understanding of fealty and homage. There is no context outlining the wider relationship between Balliol and Edward or between Scotland and England. There is almost no analysis of the 'tone' of the source, which seems to suggest that Balliol had got himself into a mess as a result of bad advice and his own foolishness and that Balliol has decided to surrender Scotland to Edward as a result of Balliol's own free will. In reality, Balliol had been chased across Scotland and was captured. He had no choice – and even less 'free will'! In essence, this answer focuses on only one part of the relationship between Balliol and Edward. There should be much more.

How many marks would it get?

The first part of the answer might gain 2 out of 4 marks. It acknowledges that the war between Scotland and England came about by Balliol breaking his feudal promises. There is some explanation of what those promises involved. Apart from the already credited information about fealty and homage, there is very little recall apart from mentions of defeat at Dunbar, Edward invading and then chasing Balliol across Scotland. At best this would get 2 out of 7 marks.

In total, this answer would gain 4 out of 10 marks, a generous mark given the shallowness of the answer.

Here's how the answer could be better.

This source only partly shows the relationship between Edward and Balliol. It deals with the war between Scotland and England prompted by the Scots alliance with France and the attack on Northern England 'which displeased and angered our lord Edward'. Edward then launched an invasion starting at Berwick where the town was sacked. After that, the Scots were defeated at Dunbar. Edward then went north, chasing the Scots. Balliol was eventually captured and his badges of office stripped from his coat, hence Balliol's nickname - toom tabard. Scotland was then taken over by Edward.

On the other hand, the source does not explain the relationship between Balliol and Edward or the feudal agreements that existed between them. Nor does the source mention how Edward chose Balliol as king of Scotland.

The Great Cause was the question of who should rule Scotland after the death of Alexander III. Balliol was one of several 'competitors' and he was chosen mainly because he was closest in succession to Alexander. Balliol did homage for Scotland and as such accepted Edward as his feudal overlord ('our lord Edward') and superior. By doing this Balliol guaranteed to support Edward when called upon to do so.

When Edward asked for help against the French, Balliol broke his oath of fealty by 'renouncing our homage'. The relationship that had been agreed - of feudal vassal and overlord - had therefore been broken.

Balliol's leadership of the Scottish army was weak and although the letter suggests that Balliol was surrendering Scotland of his own free will, the truth is that the Scots were defeated and Balliol had no choice. Edward had asserted his power and indeed his right to teach his vassal a lesson.

This source tries to sound as if Balliol has been foolish and is almost apologetic to Edward. The English invasion is described as 'something he had a right to do as lord of his fee' and Scottish actions are described as the result of 'bad and wrong advice and our own foolishness'. Given that the source was written at or near the place that Balliol was captured, then it seems as if either Balliol was told to write this or he was making a last attempt to appease Edward.

Why is this a better answer?

It sets the context and explains the wider relationship between Edward and Balliol. Appropriate vocabulary such as vassal and overlord is used. The answer is an appropriate length. There is good analysis of the content of the source. There is a great deal of accurate and relevant detail. Overall, this answer does try to evaluate how fully the source shows the relationship between Edward and Balliol.

This answer could easily gain 4 out of 4 for developing the source and could also gain 6 out of 7 for some very specific points of recall. The answer could achieve full marks: 10/10.

EXAM EXAMPLE 8

This example is from Special Topic option Scotland and the Impact of the Great War, 1914–1928.

> How fully does Source E explain the impact of the war on political developments in Scotland? Use the source and recalled knowledge part of the question.

Source E: from a speech at Glasgow City Hall against the Munitions Act in 1916 made by David Kirkwood

> *Fellow engineers, the country is at war. The country must win. In order to win, we must throw our whole soul into the production of munitions. Now we come to the point of difference. The Government and its supporters think that to get the best out of us, they must take away our liberty. So we are deprived of the chief thing that distinguishes free men from slaves, the right to leave a master when we wish to. If I work in Beardmore's I am as much his property as if he had branded a 'B' on my brow.*
>
> *Mr. Lloyd George claims that all this is necessary in order to win the War. I deny it. We are willing, as we have always been, to do our bit, but we object to slavery.*

Here is a weak answer to the question.

The Munitions Act put workers under military control and Kirkwood does not like that. During the war, the Government had to make sure they had enough munitions produced so they tried to make sure that workers could not go on strike or disrupt production. Kirkwood agrees that Britain needed to win the war but he objected to increasing Governmental control. During the war, the Government increased its control over most people's lives with changes such as rationing and conscription.

Why is this a weak answer?

It understands Kirkwood's point about governmental control but should have explained more fully the restrictions the Government placed on workers' freedom to move jobs. It makes no attempt to look at the wider issue of political changes in Scotland. The main weakness in this answer is that the candidate does not move away from the source. There should be a wider answer dealing with the impact of the war on politics in Scotland. The candidate only really makes the point about increasing government control and some workers' objection to this.

This can only get at most 2 marks out of 4. There is perhaps only one piece of recall that MIGHT gain a mark. This answer would therefore get no more than 3 marks out of 10.

This is better (but not brilliant!)

The Munitions Act put workers under military control and Kirkwood does not like that. During the war the Government had to make sure they had enough munitions produced so they tried to make sure that workers could not go on strike or disrupt production. Kirkwood agrees Britain needed to win the war but he objected to increasing Government control. During the war the Government increased its control over most people's lives with changes such as rationing and conscription.

This was one of the complaints that led to worker protest that became known as Red Clydeside. During the war some workers became supporters of socialism and the Independent Labour Party. Elsewhere the middle classes turned to the Conservative or Unionist parties to save them from possible revolution. Scotland became divided between left-wing supporters and right-wing supporters and the old fashioned Liberal Party broke in two and never had power again. The overall impact of the war was that it changed Scottish politics.

Why is this a better answer?

This answer at least brings in relevant recall. It shows an understanding of the changes in Scottish politics brought about by the war. This answer would still only gain 2 out of 4 for developing the source but could gain 4 out of 7 for relevant recall. This answer could gain a total of 6 out of 10.

EVALUATING PICTURE QUESTIONS

It is quite possible that a picture or cartoon might be used as a source within your Paper 2 Special topic. It is very unlikely that an illustration would be used as part of the comparison question, but it is possible to use an illustration in any of the other three questions.

What are the essential tips for answering this type of question?

Don't ignore the illustration. Do use the provenance (who produced it, when and where) to help you explain why it was produced.

Don't just describe the illustration. Explain the main point being made by the producer of the illustration. What thoughts or emotions did the producer want to stir in the people who saw the illustration?

Finally, do what you are asked to do. Link the illustration to the main point of the question by doing the evaluation asked in the question.

How will I know what the illustration is about?

Picture questions often require you to set a cartoon or illustration in context and then analyse it, making clear the meaning of the illustration or the intention of the artist.

What does 'setting in context' mean?

Setting in context means to explain the big event that caused the source to be produced. For example, in The Impact of the Great War on Scotland, 1914–1928, a cartoon or picture dated August 1914 will almost certainly be about Britain getting involved in the war and trying to recruit men to the army. Likewise, in The Treaty of Union, 1689–1740 an illustration from 1707 will probably be about the Treaty of Union between England and Scotland.

Other illustrations may depict wider themes within the topic, such as the example you will see later about Scottish independence.

Must I use my own knowledge in this answer?

Yes. It is never enough just to describe what you see in the illustration. You MUST use your own knowledge to develop the points in the cartoon or illustration. That means you must explain in detail the points shown or hinted at in the illustration. Write an answer long enough to make as many developed points as there are marks for the question.

EXAM EXAMPLE 9

Here is an example question from The Impact of the Great War on Scotland, 1914–1928.

Source A: a recruitment poster used in Scotland in 1914.

> How useful is this source as evidence for why so many young Scots joined the army in 1914?

This is a very weak answer.

This source is very useful. It is a primary source and is about making men join the army. Britain needed more soldiers so posters tried to persuade men to join up. The soldier in the picture looks strong and men would want to be like him. Lots of posters said the King and country needed them and men joined to help their country. The poster also says soldiers would get honour and glory. There were other reasons why men joined up such as wanting to escape boring jobs. Other people thought the war would be over by Christmas.

Why is this a weak answer?

There are 5 marks available for this question in total. There are no marks given for stating a source is primary and the rest of that paragraph is mainly a description of the source. This answer would only gain 1 out of 2. The mark given was for writing about the purpose of the source – to persuade young men to join up. There are four very clear points in the source that could be explained. This answer fails to deal with any of them. The point about wanting honour and glory is a misunderstanding of the source. This section would gain 0 marks.

This answer contains one other relevant point of recall about reasons why men joined the army – to escape boring jobs. The other comment about the war being over by Christmas is not developed and no clear connection is made between that idea and why men joined the army. This section would only gain 1 mark out of 2.

In total this answer gains 2 marks out of 5.

With a little more relevant recall or use of the source this answer could have passed easily. The reason it did not pass is that it did not follow the rules about how to answer this type of question. If you make sure you do that, a pass mark should be easy to get.

Here is a good answer.

This source is useful evidence for several reasons. First of all it is a primary source, produced by the Government in 1914 to help boost recruitment in Scotland. When war broke out it was very important to get men to join up as fast as possible. Different ways were invoked to persuade men to join. Firstly, by showing a Scottish soldier in a kilt it uses Scottish patriotism and the pride in the kilted regiments of Scotland. Secondly, the poster tells young men that their king and country needed them and that made some feel guilty if they did not join up when they were needed. Thirdly, by joining up, they could help protect the British Empire. This poster asks young men not to let down the 'honour and glory' of the Empire.

Finally, at the bottom of the poster are the words 'A wee scrap of paper is Britain's bond'. This refers to the Treaty of London in which Britain promised to protect Belgium's neutrality. Recruits felt they were keeping a promise to Belgium - their 'bond'. The word 'wee' was also deliberate.

It made the promise to Belgium seem more personal to Scots and that they should help to protect Belgium against the German bully.

On the other hand, the poster does not cover all reasons for recruitment. Some posters made the Germans seem like mad beasts that raped and destroyed. One famous poster of Kitchener is an optical illusion. The pointing finger and eyes seem to look directly at anyone who sees the poster and makes them volunteer.

Some people joined up because they thought the war would be exciting and over by Christmas. If they did not join, they would miss the fun. Others joined up either because they were unemployed or were bored in their ordinary jobs.

Overall, this poster is useful as evidence because it uses patriotism, pride in Scotland, the need to keep promises and the chance to help Belgium as ways of persuading men to join up.

Why is this a good answer?

There are 5 marks available for this question in total. You can get UP TO 2 marks for writing about the source's origin and purpose and explaining why these things are important in the context of the question. This answer does all three things.

You can get UP TO 2 marks for explaining points in the picture that are useful in terms of the question. In this case there are four features in the picture relevant to why Scots joined the army and these are thoroughly explained.

Finally, you can get UP TO 2 marks for using your own detailed knowledge as long as it is relevant to the question. In this answer there is a lot of recall explaining other reasons why Scots joined the army in 1914. These recall points also provide balanced evaluation to the question of how useful the source is. In this case the source is quite useful but does not give the full story.

This answer scores highly on all three stages of the marking scheme and gains the maximum mark of 5 out of 5.

EXAM EXAMPLE 10

This example is from study
topic Migration and Empire
1830–1939.

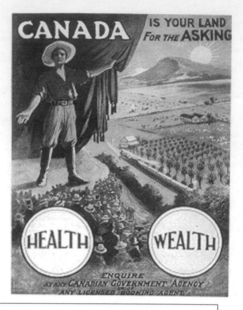

How far does this source show the reasons for which so many Scots
emigrated during the later 19th and early 20th centuries?

Here is a weak answer.

*This poster gives a good picture of life in Canada. The poster
shows that emigrants will be healthy and wealthy and can get
land easily. The poster was originally in colour and is bright
and attractive. The poster is partly useful for showing reasons
for emigration. It shows no push reasons such as hunger and
unemployment as reasons why people move.*

*The Highland Clearances was an important reason for emigration.
People were forced out of their homes by landlords who burned the
crofters' houses to force them to leave. The Highlanders were replaced
by sheep such as the black-faced Cheviot. These sheep could cope with
bad weather and made more money for landlords in the Highlands.
The poster does not show reasons for emigration to other countries.*

Why is this a weak answer?

There is no attempt to set the poster or the issue in context. This answer just
gives a very general description of the poster without explaining the main points
in it.

There is almost no relevant recall – the long section on the Highland Clearances has very little relevance to the question. There is very little balance in evaluating the 'how far' part of the question although it does comment that there are no 'push' reasons for emigration shown in the poster.

Remember, you can get up to 4 marks for identifying relevant points in the source AND explaining them. This answer only describes what is in the source so will probably gain 0 out of 4 marks for this part.

You can also get up to 7 marks for including accurate and relevant information but this answer has very little. The section on the Highland Clearances has some accurate recall and it is relevant to reasons for emigration but the information is not used as a direct answer to the question. It would have been better to write 'There were other reasons to emigrate that are not mentioned in the source such as the Highland Clearances. The Highland Clearances were...'

In total, this section would gain no more than 3 marks out of 7, making an overall total of 3 out of 10.

Here is a better answer.

Scots emigrated in search of a better life and many of them went to relatively nearby Canada. Others went further to Australia and New Zealand. Scots also migrated within Scotland and tended to move towards the more industrialised central belt. In all cases, Scots migrated essentially for two types of reasons - push and pull.

This poster was issued by the Canadian Government and promotes directly the 'pull' reasons for migration. The poster suggests emigrants will have more wealth, be healthier and can easily become landowners. The land and climate look welcoming and the crowds of people shown entering Canada prove that it is a popular destination. Finally, the train suggests that transport is easy and the settled landscape suggests safety. All these points were hugely attractive to poor, landless Scots living in the unhealthy towns and cities of Scotland.

Naturally since this is an advertising poster it will only give the positive side to emigrating to Canada but it does manage to hint at the 'push' reasons such as ill health and poverty. Throughout the 19th and early 20th centuries many Scots suffered from ill health and poverty so anything offering an escape from such a life would be welcomed. Crofters and lowland tenants forced out of farming would also be attracted by the promise of new land 'for the asking'.

Overall, this poster does touch on the main push and pull reasons for emigrating to Canada but tells us nothing about why Scots chose to emigrate to other places such as Australia and New Zealand.

Why is this a better answer?

There is a scene-setting introduction that contains important, detailed recall. The answer looks at the wider context of migration and shows knowledge of migration both abroad and within Scotland. There is identification of four reasons for emigration contained in the poster although they could have been better explained. There are at least four and probably five major pieces of accurate and relevant recall in this answer.

In total this answer should get 3/4 for using the source and 5/7 for recall gaining a total of 8 out of 10.

EXAM EXAMPLE 11

Here is an example of a picture source question from the Wars of Independence unit used in the 10 mark 'How fully' question.

How fully does this source illustrate the issues and difficulties involved in the succession problem in Scotland between 1286 and 1292?

Here is a good answer.

When Alexander III fell from his horse and was killed, Scotland faced a crisis. The only heir was Alexander's granddaughter, Margaret. When Margaret died, Scotland had no clear heir to the throne. Several Scots claimed they had a right to be king and Edward of England was asked to choose who should be king.

Edward saw his chance to become overlord of Scotland. The picture shows that difference in relationship but only partly illustrates the issues and difficulties involved in the succession problem in Scotland between 1286 and 1292.

Edward is shown seated above Balliol and looking down on him. Balliol, who was chosen as king by Edward, is shown on his knees promising to support Edward. Balliol is doing an act of homage. That was almost like a legal contract to support Edward so the source may be propaganda for the English claim to rule Scotland.

While Margaret was still alive Edward tried to arrange a marriage between her and his son so that he would gain control over Scotland. All the way through the succession crisis and the Great Cause, Edward had tried to gain influence and control over Scotland. Edward wanted to be overlord of Scotland and even called it his 'land', and not a separate country.

Now, Edward wanted to make Scotland his possession and to control the Scottish King. The advisers standing near Edward in the right corner of the picture do not look very interested in Balliol as they talk to each other. In this English painting Balliol is made to look much less important than Edward, perhaps showing how England saw its relationship with Scotland.

The picture may also help people to understand why war broke out between Scotland and England. In 1296 Balliol refused to support Edward in a war against France. As far as Edward was concerned Balliol had broken his oath of loyalty (or fealty) and had to be punished. Edward invaded Scotland and eventually captured Balliol, immediately stripping him of all his royal badges and symbols, including the crown Balliol is wearing.

Why does this answer score highly?

There are 4 marks available for selecting relevant points from the source AND for developing each point with recalled, detailed knowledge. This answer develops three points from the source well, so this section gains 3 out of 4. This answer also contains at least five other points of recall relevant to the answer and there is an attempt to provide an evaluation of 'how fully'. This section would gain at least 5 marks out of 7.

In total this answer would gain 8 out of 10.

Here is another answer to the same question. What do you think it is worth?

> When Alexander III died Scotland had no king. Eventually Edward decided John Balliol had the best claim to the throne of Scotland. In exchange Balliol was to support Edward and the picture shows King John Balliol promising to be a loyal supporter of Edward of England. Balliol had to kneel in front of Edward and promise to support him. The system of government at the time was called the feudal system and in that system Balliol would be known as 'inferior' or less important than Edward. This picture shows John Balliol doing homage and promising to be loyal to King Edward I.
>
> There is no doubt in this picture who is the most important person – Edward. He sits in a higher chair and looks more important. Balliol is lower down and that suggests that Edward thinks Scotland is his to control. That is what Edward wanted.

What do you think about this answer?

- Is the context set well?
- Is the information organised well?
- There is some relevant recall but does it need more development?
- Does the answer identify good points from the picture? Are they well explained?
- Is there a direct answer to the 'How fully' part of the question?

Thinking about marking

How many marks would you award this question? Markers ask themselves the following four questions:

- Should this answer pass (5 marks)?
- If it is a pass answer is it a good pass (8–10 marks)?
- If it is not a pass is it a bad fail (3 marks or less)?
- Is it an answer that just does not quite make half marks?

Once you have decided the answers to these questions, you can fine-tune your marks by looking closely at the marking rules.

The point of doing this is that you should apply the same thinking to your own work. Be honest – does your work deserve to pass well? If not, what are YOU going to do about it?

Conclusion

Now you are ready for your exam. Good luck.

When a famous golfer was told he had been lucky when he holed a long putt, he replied 'You know, the more I practice the luckier I get.' In other words, you don't need luck. You have worked hard and you know what to expect in the exam. Eat and sleep well before the exam. Allow plenty of time to arrive at where you will sit the exam.

Avoid arguments before the exam and also avoid hangovers! Be as relaxed as you can be.

Use time carefully and all will be well.

And what will Higher History gain you? What advantages has the study of history brought you?

In the short term, you will know a lot of facts about the topics you have learned. You will also gain a respected qualification that will assist your entry to further education or employment.

But in the longer term, perhaps you have gained more than you think. You have acquired many transferable skills, which is a major strength of Higher History.

In your Extended Essay you had to use planning, researching, organising and presenting skills.

In Paper 1, you had to work against the clock to construct an argument based on an issue. To do that you had to use your information to present a clear argument with a beginning, a middle and an end – the essential skills for any presentation you will do in your life.

In Paper 2, you had to use your skills of analysis and evaluation. Throughout life you will use such skills to arrive at informed decisions.

The facts of history are in the past but the skills you have now will equip you for the future.

Glossary

Context – this means the situation that existed when an event happened which can help explain the event.

Evaluation – in Higher History Paper 1 you are asked to evaluate opinions or ideas such as in questions which start 'How far do you agree...' or 'To what extent...'. In Paper 2 the evaluation questions will often ask how useful or how reliable a source is. In all these cases you are asked to reach a judgement based on your knowledge and skill.

Extended Essay – it counts for 30 marks out of the course total of 100. You are allowed a plan of 200 words and 2 hours to write up this essay in exam conditions.

External assessments – these are part of the final exam. Your Extended Essay, although written in your educational establishment, is sent away and marked by SQA markers. Likewise, your Higher exam – Paper 1 and Paper 2 – are sent off to be marked.

Historiography – Historians research the past by finding and using evidence to support their ideas. Often historians differ over their interpretations of past events. Historiography is the study of those differing opinions. By using your knowledge of these differing opinions you will be able to make a more effective debate-type answer.

Internal assessments – assessments carried out within your educational establishment and marked by your teacher/tutor. There are three internal assessments and each must be passed.

Issue – essay titles in Higher History are issue based. That means they present an idea or opinion to you and it is up to you to use your knowledge to argue for or against the idea.

Paper 1 – the first exam paper you will sit as part of your Higher exam. It lasts for 80 minutes and in that time you must write two essays, each on a different unit.

Paper 2 – the second exam paper you will sit as part of your Higher exam. It lasts for 85 minutes and in that time you must answer four questions based on sources relevant to your Special Study.

Primary source – any source produced around the time of the event described or shown in the source. Primary sources can include opinions or descriptions written by people who were alive at the time but who produce the source later – such as autobiographies or memoirs based on diaries kept at the time.

Secondary source – a source produced by someone not directly involved in the events they describe and usually many years later. Historians producing secondary sources such as a textbook use primary sources and hindsight to form opinions about the past based on the available evidence.

Syllabus – the exact content of your Higher History course is available on the SQA website. The syllabus defines exactly what could be in your final exam. Each year the syllabus is sampled in the exam. This means that some topics will be left out.

Word count – your Extended Essay plan must be no longer than 200 words. You must state an accurate word count on your plan.